Jossey-Bass Teacher

Jossey-Bass Teacher provides K–12 teachers with essential knowledge and tools to create a positive and lifelong impact on student learning. Trusted and experienced educational mentors offer practical classroom-tested and theory-based teaching resources for improving teaching practice in a broad range of grade levels and subject areas. From one educator to another, we want to be your first source to make every day your best day in teaching. *Jossey-Bass Teacher* resources serve two types of informational needs—essential knowledge and essential tools.

Essential knowledge resources provide the foundation, strategies, and methods from which teachers may design curriculum and instruction to challenge and excite their students. Connecting theory to practice, essential knowledge books rely on a solid research base and time-tested methods, offering the best ideas and guidance from many of the most experienced and well-respected experts in the field.

Essential tools save teachers time and effort by offering proven, ready-to-use materials for in-class use. Our publications include activities, assessments, exercises, instruments, games, ready reference, and more. They enhance an entire course of study, a weekly lesson, or a daily plan. These essential tools provide insightful, practical, and comprehensive materials on topics that matter most to K–12 teachers.

Hands-On Science Mysteries for Grades 3–6

Standards-Based Inquiry Investigations

James Robert Taris
Louis James Taris

JOSSEY-BASS
A Wiley Imprint
www.josseybass.com

Published by Jossey-Bass
A Wiley Imprint
989 Market Street, San Francisco, CA 94103-1741   www.josseybass.com

Jossey-Bass books and products are available through most bookstores. To contact Jossey-Bass directly call our Customer Care Department within the U.S. at 800-956-7739, outside the U.S. at 317-572-3986, or fax 317-572-4002.

Jossey-Bass also publishes its books in a variety of electronic formats. Some content that appears in print may not be available in electronic books.

Library of Congress Cataloging-in-Publication Data
Taris, James Robert, 1943-
Hands-on science mysteries for grades 3-6: standards-based inquiry investigations / James Robert Taris, Louis James Taris.—1st ed.
p. cm.—(Jossey-bass teacher)
Includes bibliographical references and index.
ISBN-13: 978-0-471-69760-2 (alk. paper)
ISBN-10: 0-471-69760-5 (alk. paper)
1. Science—Miscellanea—Juvenile literature. 2. Science—Experiments—Juvenile literature. 3. Science—Study and teaching (Elementary)—United States. I. Taris, Louis James, 1930- II. Title. III. Series.
Q163.T245 2006
372.35'044—dc22
2006009131

Printed in the United States of America
FIRST EDITION
PB Printing   10 9 8 7 6 5 4 3 2 1

About This Book

Hands-On Science Mysteries for Grades 3–6 is a lab-based ancillary program for students that is designed to support the National Science Standards on many levels.

First, the activities are all rooted in inquiry. The lab investigations are designed to pique students' curiosity and lead them to examine mysterious phenomena in an orderly fashion. The labs are constructed to encourage the development of science inquiry, so students must observe, take notes, make diagrams, interpret data, and arrive at solutions.

Second, the *Hands-On Science Mysteries* program develops students' problem-solving and critical thinking skills by presenting different types of intriguing mysteries and challenging exercises.

Third, *Hands-On Science Mysteries* uses experimentation to teach basic science concepts such as static electricity, simple machines, density, optics, combustion, the use of basic science equipment, states of matter, heat, and much more.

Fourth, *Hands-On Science Mysteries* connects science to real-world situations by investigating actual mysteries or mysterious phenomena. In leaving some of the mysteries open ended, it allows students to arrive at their own explanations for these strange happenings. And each activity includes at least one extension for further investigation.

Finally, it's worth noting that for most of these labs, you will only need common everyday items found around the classroom or home, not expensive science equipment.

This program is an exciting way to get kids involved in the process of hands-on experimenting, critical thinking, problem solving, and gathering general knowledge. In other words, it makes "doing science" fun and rewarding!

About the Authors

James Robert Taris is a science teacher of twenty-five-plus years and has taught a variety of junior high, middle school, and high school science programs. Mr. Taris has also been a science coordinator and has designed and taught over fifteen science teacher training programs at the college level. He has also been an educational consultant, educational grant writer, research assistant at Harvard University Gordon McKay Laboratory of Applied Science, contributor to the *Middle School Journal,* presenter at numerous regional science conferences, designer of interdisciplinary science programs, and author and coauthor of many science education publications.

Louis James Taris is an educational consultant and a prolific writer. He is a graduate of the Boston University College of Arts and Sciences. He graduated with honors and was elected to Phi Beta Kappa, the distinguished honor society. Dr. Taris also received the degrees of Master of the Arts and Master of Education from Boston University. He later earned his Doctor of Education degree at Boston University.

Dr. Taris held the faculty position of full professor of education at Bridgewater State College, Bridgewater, Massachusetts. He was the superintendent of schools of two large school districts in Maine and Massachusetts, and has also held the positions of director of science, grades one through twelve, and director of curriculum and instruction, kindergarten through grade twelve. He has taught at the elementary, secondary, and college levels.

Dr. Taris has conducted many workshops and in-service programs for teachers and administrators, and he has spoken at state, regional, and national conferences. He is a member of the International Brotherhood of Magicians.

Acknowledgments

We extend special thanks to Mary Jane Taris, who word processed much of the text and provided editing and research assistance. We extend thanks also to JoAnn Taris, who visited sites to investigate and verify mysteries.

We thank the members of the family who provided computer work and other assistance.

Jim Taris would like to acknowledge his brother, Lou, for introducing him to the world of "Lions, Tigers, and Trained Fleas" many years ago!

Finally, we extend our gratitude to Kate C. Bradford, senior editor at Jossey-Bass, for her insights and her recommendations.

Contents

Contents

*We dedicate this work to the memory of our parents,
James and Judith Taris.*

Preface

OK, Houston. Hey, we've had a problem here.

This message was sent on April 13, 1970, from Odyssey, the Apollo 13 Command Module, which was in space, to NASA's Mission Control in Houston, Texas. An explosion had occurred in the service module, where cylinders of liquid oxygen were stored. It was now impossible for LEM, the lunar entry module, to separate from the spacecraft and land an astronaut on the moon. There was also a distinct possibility that the spacecraft and its crew of three would be trapped permanently in space.

Over a period of 87 hours and 57 minutes at Mission Control and the Kennedy Space Center, some heavy-duty critical thinking and problem solving took place. The scientists at Mission Control had to forget all of their carefully made plans for the mission and work out a creative new way to make it possible for the seriously damaged spacecraft to return to the earth safely.

Critical and creative thinking are cornerstones of science and are significant tools for solving problems. *Hands-On Science Mysteries for Grades 3–6: Standards-Based Inquiry Investigations* is written to be a teacher's partner. It is designed to let teachers introduce high-interest problems and problem-solving situations to help young people develop and hone their ability to solve problems. As they solve these problems, students will be learning about basic science concepts and science principles.

Throughout the Apollo 13 crisis, Mission Control and the Kennedy Space Center squarely addressed complex, highly technical problems and solved them successfully. It is our hope that the young people who are reached by the teachers who use this book will master the skills of solving problems just as effectively while they grow in their knowledge and understanding of science.

James Robert Taris
Louis James Taris

1. The Mystery of the Bed of Nails

An Indian *fakir* (a Hindu magician) sets out a bed of nails in front of his audience. He inflates a balloon and drops it on the bed of nails. It pops. The fakir then lies down on the bed of nails and has several spectators stand on him. After the spectators have returned to the audience, the fakir stands and turns his back to the spectators. There are no puncture wounds from the nails. The fakir is unharmed! How can this be possible? Think of a skier crossing very deep snow. If the skier were to remove his skis and try to walk in the snow, what would happen? What do these two situations have in common?

Lab: Can You Stand the Pressure?

In this lab, we will examine the effect of surface area on how much weight can be supported.

Materials

Ruler

Pencil

Sheet of 8×12 copy paper

Scissors

Cellophane tape or masking tape

Heavy textbook

What to Do

1. Using a pencil and ruler, measure and draw six 2-inch by 6-inch rectangles on the copy paper.
2. Cut out each rectangle.
3. Roll each rectangle into a tube and fasten with the tape.
4. Place the six tubes (evenly spaced) on end and on a flat surface.
5. Place the textbook on the six paper tubes. Observe.
6. Remove the book and all but one of the tubes from the flat surface. Place the center of the book onto the single tube. Observe.

Bed of Nails *(Continued)*

Describe Your Results

1. What happened when you placed the heavy book on the six evenly spaced paper tubes?

   _____

   _____

2. What happened when you placed the book on the single tube?

   _____

   _____

3. What is the advantage of using many paper tubes?

   _____

   _____

What's the Solution?

Now that you have completed the lab, use what you have discovered to solve "The Mystery of the Bed of Nails."

Bed of Nails *(Continued)*

Exercises

Fill in the blanks with the correct answer:

1. A fakir is a Hindu _____ .
2. A fakir lies on a bed of _____ .
3. The fakir asks several spectators to _____ on him.
4. The fakir does not get puncture_____ from the nails.

True or False?

1. Fakirs come from Japan. _____
2. The fakir drops a balloon on the nails, which does not pop.
   _____
3. The fakir is unharmed by the nails. _____
4. Skis prevent skiers from sinking into the snow. _____

Unscramble these words from the activity:

1. UPNCTERU _____
2. DWNUO _____
3. ILAN _____
4. RKIFA _____
5. IKS _____

Extension

How would using a surfboard be similar to what you have learned from this activity?

2. The Mystery of the High Wire Walker

In 1859, The Great Blondin (Jean François Gravelot) became the first daredevil to walk across Niagara Falls on a tightrope. The rope was 1,100 feet in length and three inches in diameter. It stretched across the Falls from Niagara Falls, New York, to Niagara Falls, Ontario, Canada. The Great Blondin completed the crossing in twenty minutes.

For many years there have been a few brave people who have walked across thin ropes and wires (sometimes hundreds of feet in the air) between skyscrapers and even across deep canyons. How do these daring people accomplish this dangerous and seemingly impossible feat of balance?

Lab: A Long Way Down

In this lab, we will examine how an object's ability to balance is affected by the distribution of weight. How does changing the location of some of the weight help an object balance?

Materials

Boy template

Tagboard

Scissors

Pliers or wire cutters

Metal wire hanger (or suitable flexible wire)

Modeling clay

Glue or tape

18-inch length of string

Two chairs

What to Do

1. Cut out the paper boy template.
2. Trace the template onto the sheet of tagboard.
3. Cut out the tagboard boy.
4. Using pliers or wire cutters, cut 12 inches of hanger wire and bend this wire into a semicircular shape.
5. Glue or tape the wire across the hands of the boy cutout so that the wire ends are drooping down.

High Wire Walker *(Continued)*

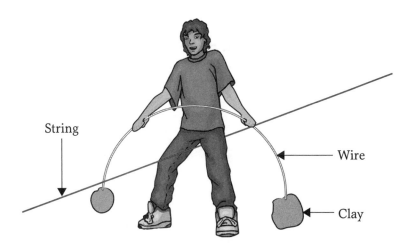

String

Wire

Clay

6. Fasten two balls of modeling clay to the ends of the wire.

7. Tie the 18-inch length of string between two chairs so that the string is taut.

8. Balance the boy on the string and observe.

9. Remove the clay from the wire and try to balance the boy.

10. Replace the modeling clay and observe.

Describe Your Results

1. What happened to the boy in step 8?

_____

_____

2. What happened when you removed the clay from the wire in step 9?

_____

_____

3. From your observations, what effect do the clay balls and wire have on the boy as it balances on the string?

_____

_____

High Wire Walker *(Continued)*

What's the Solution?

Now that you have completed the lab, use what you discovered to solve "The Mystery of the High Wire Walker." Additional hint: It has to do with something called the *center of balance*.

Exercises

Fill in the blanks with the correct answer:

1. The Great _____ walked across Niagara Falls on a tightrope.
2. The rope was 1,100 feet in length and _____ in diameter.
3. Niagara Falls is in both New York and _____, Canada.
4. Tightrope walking is a dangerous feat of _____.

True or False?

1. High wire walkers also walk on ropes. _____
2. A high wire walker does not need good balance. _____
3. Niagara Falls is in Australia. _____
4. A clue to this mystery is center of motion. _____

Unscramble these words from the activity:

1. EWRI _____
2. IGHH _____
3. ABACELN _____
4. WRKAEL _____
5. LLFA _____

Extension

What do you think would happen if you made the boy's wire longer?

3. The Mystery of the Brooklyn Bridge Disease

The Brooklyn Bridge, connecting Brooklyn and Manhattan, was built during the nineteenth century. Its completion was heralded as one of the wonders of the modern world. To build the bridge, *pilings* (large, long, stone columns) had to be sunk down to the bedrock below the mud and silt of the East River. These pilings would support the towers from which the bridge would be suspended.

A *caisson* (a dam that would hold back the river water) was built so that workmen could make the pilings. Workers called *sandhogs* entered the caisson and tunneled down to the bedrock to set the bridge supports. They worked in tunnels at depths of 80 feet or more under the river's water! At these depths, there is very high pressure. After working for a short time, many of the sandhogs began to complain of ringing ears, dizziness, and headaches.

Several of the sandhogs became sick with a painful disease that paralyzed them and even killed some of them. What caused this strange illness that almost stopped the building of the Brooklyn Bridge?

Lab: Tiny Bubbles

In this lab, we will examine what happens to raisins and grapes that are immersed in clear carbonated soda. Carbonated drinks are made by dissolving carbon dioxide gas under pressure in water or a water-based liquid. When the pressure is decreased, as when you take the cap off of a bottle of soda, bubbles of carbon dioxide are released. How might bubbles have affected the sandhogs working on the Brooklyn Bridge?

Materials

Clear carbonated soda	Raisins
Glass tumbler	Several grapes

What to Do

1. Fill a glass tumbler with clear carbonated soda.
2. Place several raisins into the liquid and observe what happens.
3. Now place a grape into the liquid and observe what happens.
4. Peel the skin from a grape using your fingernails or a knife.
5. Place the peeled grape into the liquid and observe what happens.

Brooklyn Bridge
Disease *(Continued)*

Describe Your Results

1. What happened to the raisins in the soft drink?

   _____

   _____

2. What happened to the whole grape when it was placed in the carbonated soda?

   _____

   _____

3. What happened to the peeled grape when it was placed into the liquid?

   _____

   _____

4. What did you see forming on the raisins and peeled grape?

   _____

   _____

5. Why do you think this happened?

   _____

   _____

What's the Solution?

Now that you have completed the lab, use what you discovered to solve "The Mystery of the Brooklyn Bridge disease." Additional hints: The name of the disease is Caisson's disease, and it has to do with changes in a person's bloodstream.

Brooklyn Bridge
Disease *(Continued)*

Exercises

Fill in the blanks with the correct answer:

1. The name of the bridge that the sandhogs were building is

   _____ .

2. Another name for the Brooklyn Bridge disease is

   _____ .

3. Working at 80 feet below the surface of the river meant the workers were under _____ pressure.

4. In the experiment the _____ stuck to the raisins and the unpeeled grape, causing them to rise and fall.

True or False?

1. Sandhogs work deep underground and under high pressure.

   _____

2. Caissons allow workers to work under water. _____

3. The Brooklyn Bridge connects Brooklyn to Boston.

   _____

4. Sandhogs working on the Brooklyn Bridge never became sick.

   _____

Unscramble these words from the activity:

1. OBKRONYL _____
2. NRISAI _____
3. EDGIRB _____
4. NPIA _____
5. SGA _____

Extension

Find out more about Caisson's disease. What was the gas involved, and how can the disease be prevented?

Name _____   Date _____

4. The Mystery of the Magician's Flame

A magician walks out onto a stage. Suddenly he points at his audience and a huge flame shoots out of his finger. He repeats this throughout his performance to the amazement of onlookers. Many great magicians of the past, such as Chung Ling Soo and Harry Blackstone, have performed this type of illusion. How does the magician make such a large flame seemingly out of nothing?

Lab: Poof! (Teacher Demonstration)

In this lab, we will examine the effect of blowing a little cornstarch into a candle flame by using a straw.

Materials

Protective goggles	Cornstarch
Candle	Spoon
Matches	Drinking straw

What to Do

1. Wearing protective goggles, the teacher should light the candle.
2. Take a spoonful of cornstarch and dump it onto the candle flame. Observe.
3. Place a little cornstarch in one end of the straw. Explain to the class that this should never be attempted at home. It is strictly a demonstration done under controlled conditions—a fireproof classroom!
4. Being careful not to scorch your spectators, blow the cornstarch into the flame. Observe.

Describe Your Results

1. Why do experiments with fire have to be limited to a special place such as the classroom?

   _____

   _____

2. Why is it important to wear protective goggles when experimenting with flames?

   _____

   _____

Magician's Flame *(Continued)*

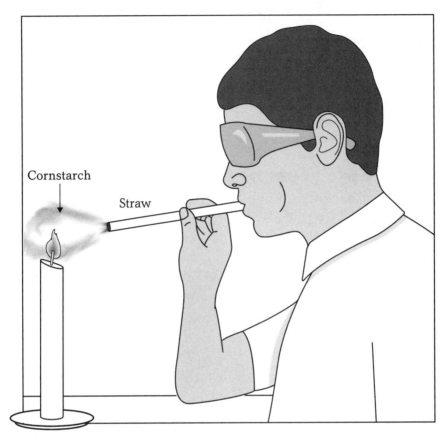

Cornstarch

Straw

3. What happened to the candle flame when the spoonful of corn-starch was dumped on it?

_____

_____

4. What happened when the drinking straw was used to blow the cornstarch across the flame?

_____

_____

5. Explain the difference between step 3 and step 4.

_____

_____

Magician's Flame *(Continued)*

What's the Solution?

Now that you have completed the lab, use what you discovered to solve "The Mystery of the Magician's Flame." Additional hint: Cornstarch, which comes from a plant, can be flammable.

Exercises

Fill in the blanks with the correct answer:

1. Many famous magicians have performed _____ like this one.
2. In this illusion, _____ seems to come from the magician's fingers.
3. When experimenting with flame, one should always wear protective _____.
4. Cornstarch comes from _____.

True or False?

1. Famous magicians like Houdini often used fire to amaze their audiences. _____
2. Experiments with fire have to be performed in safe places such as a fireproof classroom. _____
3. Cornstarch can be flammable. _____

Unscramble these words from the activity:
1. TPLNA _____
2. WASTR _____
3. EMLFA _____
4. CSHCTRONAR _____
5. SIULNLOI _____

Extension

Is flour flammable? Repeat the same experiment using several brands of flour.

5. The Mystery of the Desert Mirage

For many years desert travelers have encountered strange sights called mirages as they traveled across the desert. Cities, mountains, trees, rivers, travelers on camels, and large lakes are just a few of the sights that might appear and disappear as the desert traveler watches in awe!

The "Lakes of Satan" have been seen to appear and disappear on the Sahara Desert in Africa. The Bedouin people of this region warn travelers not to wander off in search of these elusive pools of water. Doing so, they say, will only result in becoming lost in the shifting sands of the desert.

How does this strange phenomenon happen?

Lab: Where Did It Go?

In this lab, we will examine some optical illusions. An *optical illusion* is anything that deceives the human eye into seeing something that isn't real.

Materials

Glass tumbler

Water

Pencil

Cardboard tube (paper towel or toilet paper tube)

What to Do

Activity 1

1. Place the glass tumbler with water on a flat surface.

2. Place the pencil in the water.

3. View the pencil in the water at eye level. Observe.

Desert Mirage *(Continued)*

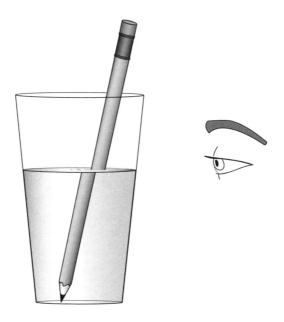

Activity 2

1. Place the tips of your index fingers together.

2. With the tips of your fingers still together, hold your hands out at arm's length and on a level with your eyes.

3. Slowly draw the fingers toward your eyes while staring at your fingertips. Observe.

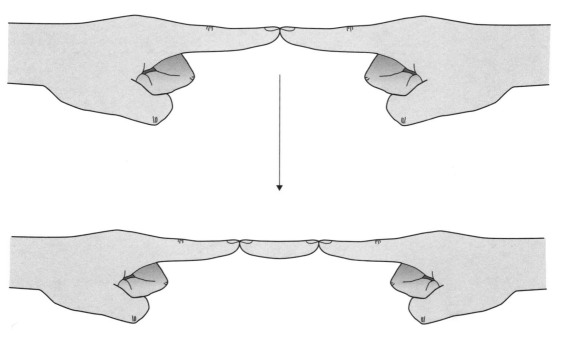

Desert Mirage *(Continued)*

Activity 3

1. Place the cardboard tube up to one eye and look at a distant object.

2. Bring your free hand up to and next to the tube and observe.

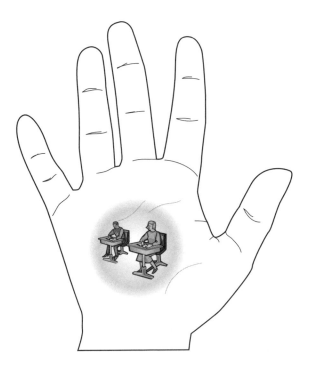

Describe Your Results

1. What did you observe in Activity 1?

_____

_____

2. What did you observe in Activity 2?

_____

_____

3. What did you observe in Activity 3?

_____

_____

Desert Mirage *(Continued)*

What's the Solution?

Now that you have completed the lab, use what you discovered to solve "The Mystery of the Desert Mirage." Additional hint: When the air near Earth's surface is very warm, light rays from the Sun can be bent, or refracted.

Exercises

Fill in the blanks with the correct answer:

1. Seeing something that is not really there is a(n)

   _____

2. Seeing something that is not really there in the desert is called a

   _____ .

3. The "Lakes of Satan" are seen in the _____ desert.

4. The _____ people warn travelers not to search for the "Lakes of Satan."

5. Our atmosphere can _____ light.

True or False?

1. Mirages are seen in deserts. _____

2. The Lakes of Satan are real lakes. _____

3. The hole in the hand activity is an optical illusion.

   _____

4. Refracted light is unbent. _____

Unscramble these words from the activity:

1. EMGIRA _____

2. TDEESR _____

3. LGHTI _____

4. AHSAAR _____

5. RIA _____

Extension

Mirages even occur over water. The most famous mirage in the world is the Fata Morgana. What is this fantastic phenomenon?

6. The Mystery of the Human Cannonball

A huge cannon has been rolled out to one side of the circus arena. Hugo Zacchini, the "Human Cannonball," dressed in bright clothes and wearing a helmet with goggles, carefully squeezes himself into the mouth of the large cannon. His audience gasps as the cannon booms and shoots the "human cannonball" across the circus arena into a large net! The audience applauds as the colorful performer jumps unharmed from the net! Hugo and the members of his family performed for many years as the grand finale of the Ringling Brothers circus. During the 1930s, Hugo and his brother Mario were shot out of a repeater cannon that shot one right after the other. The act became even more astounding when they had themselves shot over two Ferris wheels!

How could anyone survive being shot out of a cannon?

Lab: Kapow!

In this lab, we will examine a method for propelling an object from a cannon-like device.

Materials

Cotton balls

Several elastics of different sizes

Cellophane tape or masking tape

Paper towel or toilet paper tube

What to Do

1. Cut one of the elastic bands with the scissors.

2. Tape one end of the elastic band to an open end of the paper tube.

3. Position the other end of the elastic on the opposite edge of the same end of the tube, so the rest of the elastic droops two-thirds of the way into the paper tube.

4. Place a cotton ball into the tube onto the drooping elastic.

5. Point the end of the tube away from people. Grab the cotton ball and elastic and pull back and let go to shoot the cotton ball.

6. Experiment with different lengths of elastic to see which makes your cotton ball go the farthest.

7. Have a contest with your classmates to see whose "cannon" shoots the farthest distance.

Human Cannonball *(Continued)*

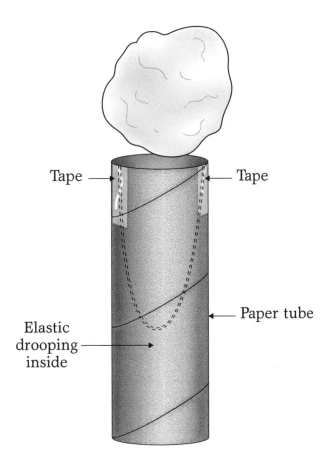

Tape — Tape

Paper tube

Elastic drooping inside

Describe Your Results

1. What happened when you shot the cotton ball?

   _____

   _____

2. What effect did using different lengths of elastic have on the distance that the cotton ball traveled?

   _____

   _____

3. After the contest, describe what made the best cannon.

   _____

   _____

Human Cannonball (Continued)

What's the Solution?

Now that you have completed the lab, use what you discovered to solve "The Mystery of the Human Cannonball." Additional hint: This device is a type of catapult.

Exercises

Fill in the blanks with the correct answer:

1. _____ was a famous human cannonball.
2. The human cannonball was caught by a large _____ .
3. Hugo and his brother Mario were once shot over two

   _____ .

4. In the lab, the cotton balls represent _____ .

True or False?

1. Hugo Zacchini and his brother were shot over a roller coaster.

   _____

2. The human cannonball was a popular circus act.

   _____

3. The human cannonball did his act without a net.

   _____

4. Hugo performed in the famous Ringling Brothers circus.

   _____

Unscramble these words from the activity:

1. TAPUCATL _____
2. HNMAU _____
3. CLEAIST _____
4. NNNCOA _____
5. STOHO _____

Extension

Draw and label a diagram showing how to shoot a human cannonball out of a cannon.

7. The Mystery of the Bermuda Triangle

The region known as the Bermuda Triangle, also called the Devil's Triangle, forms a large triangular area off the coast of Florida and stretches southward into the Caribbean Ocean. This stretch of ocean is the site of many strange happenings. Countless ships have mysteriously disappeared in this patch of water.

On March 4, 1910, the U.S.S. *Cyclops*, a large navy transport ship that was operating off the east coast of the United States, left the island of Barbados on her way to Baltimore, Maryland. Her voyage would take her through the Bermuda Triangle. The U.S.S. *Cyclops*, with 306 crew and passengers, disappeared without a trace. The U.S.S. *Cyclops* was a very large ship for its time. It also was carrying a heavy cargo of manganese ore.

Can you discover why the U.S.S. *Cyclops* and so many other ships might have vanished from this region?

Lab: Glub! Glub!

In this lab, we will examine the principle of buoyancy and how it keeps ships afloat.

Materials

Small amount of modeling clay

Beaker or plastic tumbler

Water

What to Do

1. Form a small ball of modeling clay.
2. Fill your container with water and place the clay ball on the surface of the water. Observe. Remove the clay ball from the water.
3. Take the small portion of modeling clay and fashion a small boat out of it. Make sure that its sides are high enough so that water doesn't get in the boat.
4. Float the clay boat on the surface of the water.
5. Place the small clay ball into the middle of the clay boat. Observe.
6. Swish the beaker or tumbler around so that some water gets into the clay boat. Observe.

Bermuda Triangle *(Continued)*

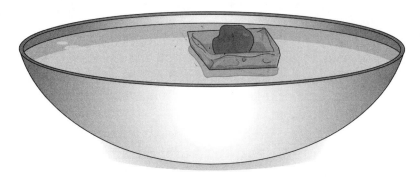

Describe Your Results

1. What did you observe when the small clay ball was placed on the water?

   _____

   _____

2. What did you observe when the clay boat was placed on the water?

   _____

   _____

3. What happened when the small clay ball was placed into the floating clay boat?

   _____

   _____

4. What happened when water was splashed into the floating clay boat?

   _____

   _____

What's the Solution?

Now that you have completed the lab, use what you discovered to solve "The Mystery of the Bermuda Triangle." Additional hint: Powerful storms have been known to develop quickly in the Bermuda Triangle, bringing high winds and huge waves.

Bermuda Triangle *(Continued)*

Exercises

Fill in the blanks with the correct answers:

1. The Bermuda Triangle is also known as the _____ Triangle.
2. The Bermuda Triangle stretches from the coast of _____ to the Caribbean Ocean.
3. Many _____ have disappeared in the Bermuda Triangle.
4. Powerful storms often occur in the _____.
5. The principle of _____ explains why boats float.

True or False?

1. The Bermuda Triangle is also called Satan's Triangle.
   _____
2. The Bermuda Triangle is in the middle of the Pacific Ocean.
   _____
3. The USS *Cyclops* was a cruise ship. _____
4. The USS *Cyclops* disappeared in 1910. _____
5. The waves in the Bermuda Triangle can be quite large.
   _____

Unscramble these words from the activity:

1. REMUBAD _____
2. ISHPS _____
3. ANTIRLGE _____
4. CLCYPOS _____
5. ADSPPEDREIA _____

Extension

What causes the huge waves sometimes called "rogue" waves?

8. The Mystery of the Booming Desert

The Sahara Desert, located in Northern Africa, is a huge expanse of shifting sands that covers an area of more than three million square miles. Visitors to this vast wasteland have sometimes heard thunderous booms accompanied by the shaking of the ground beneath their feet. What is it that causes this surprising phenomenon in a place where there are no automobiles, no cities, no people, just sand and fair weather?

Lab: Squeek!

In this lab, we will examine the composition of sand.

Materials

Small paper cup

Beach sand

Two pieces of white copy paper

Water

Eyedropper

What to Do

1. Place a small amount of beach sand in the paper cup.

2. Shake the cup. Listen carefully.

3. Put more sand into the cup.

4. Shake the cup again. Listen carefully.

5. Repeat this process one more time.

6. Spread a small amount of sand onto the white copy paper on a flat surface. Place the second sheet on top of it and gently rub it back and forth. Listen carefully.

7. Remove the top sheet and form a little mound of sand in the middle of the white copy paper. Place a few drops of water on top of the sand. Observe what happens to the water.

Booming Desert *(Continued)*

Describe Your Results

1. What did you observe when you shook the small amount of sand in the paper cup?

   _____

   _____

2. What happened when you placed more sand into the paper cup and gently shook the cup?

   _____

   _____

3. What did you observe when the sand was rubbed between the two pieces of copy paper?

   _____

   _____

4. What happened to the drops of water when they were placed on the small mound of sand?

   _____

   _____

5. What do you think is between the particles of sand?

   _____

   _____

What's the Solution?

Now that you have completed the lab, use what you discovered to solve "The Mystery of the Booming Desert." Additional hint: Dry sand is composed of both sand and air.

Booming Desert *(Continued)*

Exercises

Fill in the blanks with the correct answer:

1. The Sahara Desert is located in _____ .
2. The Sahara is a huge expanse of _____ sands.
3. Sometimes people in the Sahara have heard _____ .
4. When the booming is heard, the ground also _____ .

True or False?

1. The Sahara Desert is a huge expanse of wet sand.
   _____

2. The Sahara Desert covers an area less than 3 million square miles.
   _____

3. When dry sand is shaken in a cup, it makes a noise.
   _____

4. Dry sand is only made of sand particles. _____

Unscramble these words from the activity:

1. DSNA _____
2. MBOO _____
3. AASHRA _____
4. EDSRET _____
5. DSUON _____

Extension

Things such as cookies and cereal are sold by net weight rather than volume. Why would it be a problem to sell these products by volume?

9. The Mystery of the Loch Ness Monster

Loch Ness is a deep cold lake located in Scotland in Northern Britain. For many hundreds of years there have been stories of monsters or strange creatures in the Loch. During the last century the monster sightings have steadily increased. Many photographs and even amateur videos have been taken of the creature known affectionately as "Nessie."

Nessie is described as having a long body with flippers and a large snake-like head with breathing holes located on top. This description is similar to a prehistoric dinosaur-like creature called a plesiosaur, which inhabited the oceans and became extinct millions of years ago.

Because Loch Ness is so deep, scientists haven't been able to confirm that any of the Nessie sightings are real by direct observation. Instead they have been using the scientific method to investigate this strange mystery.

Lab: The Black Box

In this lab, we'll examine how scientists use the scientific method to identify things that they cannot see.

Materials

Black boxes

Mystery objects from around the classroom (some good objects might be pencils, scissors, chalk, markers, erasers, and so forth)

Drawing paper

Pencil

What to Do

1. The teacher should put one or two objects from around the classroom in each box before the class.

2. Each student is given a sealed black box with these instructions: There are one or two mystery objects in the box. You may not open, squeeze, or harm the box in any way. Try to figure out what is in the box.

Loch Ness Monster *(Continued)*

3. Try these experiments. By carefully moving the box (gently shaking, tipping, listening, sliding, revolving, spinning), try to guess the size and shape of the objects in the box.

4. Draw a labeled diagram of the objects you think might be in the box in the space provided. Make sure your diagram reflects the size and shape in relation to the box.

5. Open the box to see what is inside.

Describe Your Results

1. How many objects did you think were in your box?

    _____

    _____

2. Which of the movements did you find most helpful in investigating your box?

    _____

    _____

3. How much did your drawing look like the actual object in the box?

    _____

    _____

4. The four-step scientific method is (1) Identify the problem, (2) make a prediction, (3) experiment and observe, (4) find a solution. Which part of the scientific method would be most useful in solving this mystery?

    _____

    _____

What's the Solution?

Now that you have completed the lab, use what you discovered to solve "The Mystery of the Loch Ness Monster." Additional hint: Some mysteries are still waiting to be solved!

Loch Ness Monster *(Continued)*

Exercises

Fill in the blanks with the correct answer:

1. Loch Ness is a deep cold _____ in Scotland.
2. The unknown creature that inhabits the Loch is nicknamed _____.
3. This creature is described as having a long body with _____ and a snake-like head with breathing holes at the top.
4. A plesiosaur is a prehistoric _____ creature.
5. Experiment and observation is part of the _____ .

True or False?

1. The creature called "Nessie" resembles a plesiosaur.
   _____
2. Scientists use the scientific method to investigate "Nessie."
   _____
3. The black box lab is an example of how scientists try to identify something they cannot see. _____
4. The first step of the scientific method is to experiment.
   _____

Unscramble these words from the activity:

1. BXO _____
2. IENSSE _____
3. CETNSICFII _____
4. SSNE _____
5. CLHO _____

Extension

Find out what a plesiosaur looks like and draw a diagram of this ancient creature.

10. The Mystery of the Flying Rods

In Midway, New Mexico, there is a large, deep, and wide cave into which parachutists jump. During the 1990s, on one of these jumps, a parachute jumper videotaped the other parachute jumpers. Later when viewing the video, he saw strange winged shapes that seemed to be flying around the jumpers as they descended into the cave. When the video is played on slow motion one can definitely see these strange flying rods! He tried shooting another video with a different camera and got the same results. What were these weird flying rods?

Lab: An Invisible Subject

In this lab, we will examine the effects of magnetism on objects such as iron filings and videotape.

Materials

Two small rectangular kitchen magnets

Cellophane tape

Iron filings

Two pieces of white copy paper

Old discarded videotape

Scissors

What to Do

1. Place the magnet in the center of a piece of white copy paper.

2. Cover the magnet completely with cellophane tape.

3. Sprinkle some iron filings over the taped magnet. Do not jostle the magnet and iron filings. Observe.

4. Cut a small piece of videotape and place it on a piece of white copy paper.

5. Bring a small rectangular kitchen magnet close to the videotape. Observe.

Flying Rods *(Continued)*

Describe Your Results

1. Describe what happened when the iron filings were sprinkled on the magnet.

   _____

   _____

2. In this space, draw what you saw:

3. Describe what happened to the videotape when the small kitchen magnet was brought near it.

   _____

   _____

What's the Solution?

Now that you have completed the lab, use what you discovered to solve "The Mystery of the Flying Rods." Additional hints: Videotapes are made with magnetic material. All compasses have a needle that points to the North magnetic pole because it lines up with the earth's magnetic lines of force.

Exercises

Fill in the blanks with the correct answer:

1. The large cave is located in _____, New Mexico.
2. People jump into the cave wearing _____ .
3. The video showed _____ around the jumpers.
4. All compasses point _____ .

Flying Rods *(Continued)*

True or False?

1. The Flying Rods in New Mexico were seen on videotape.
   _____

2. The Flying Rods are wing-shaped. _____

3. The Flying Rods could be seen when the video was played in slow motion. _____

4. Videotapes are made with magnetic materials. _____

Unscramble these words from the activity:

1. CGAMTENI _____
2. SSMOPAC _____
3. SNWIG _____
4. OSDR _____
5. YGFILN _____

Extension

A magnet has a north pole (end) and south pole (end). Use two small kitchen magnets, one of which has been labeled N (north) and S (south) and the other has not been labeled, to discover what the Magnetic Law is.

11. The Mystery of the Raining Frogs

In London, England, in 1844, people held out their hats to catch dozens of falling frogs! In June 1997, it rained frogs in Sineola, Mexico. Over the centuries there have been numerous reports of frogs dropping from the skies. What causes this strange phenomenon?

Lab: Spinning Water

Waterspouts are tornadoes that occur over water. Though they are usually only about 2 feet in diameter, on rare occasions they can be quite large, stretching hundreds of feet into the air and reaching speeds of 200 mph! In this lab, we will examine the behavior of spinning water.

Materials

Tornado Tube (an inexpensive item that can be purchased at toy stores or science catalog companies)

Water

Two empty, clear 2-liter bottles

What to Do

1. Fill one of the 2-liter bottles with water.
2. Screw one end of the Tornado Tube onto the 2-liter bottle filled with water.
3. Screw the empty 2-liter bottle onto the open end of the Tornado Tube.
4. Set the bottles upright with the water-filled bottle on top.
5. Holding the top bottle (do not squeeze), swirl the water in a circular motion. Observe.
6. Rotate the bottles in the opposite direction and observe.

Raining Frogs *(Continued)*

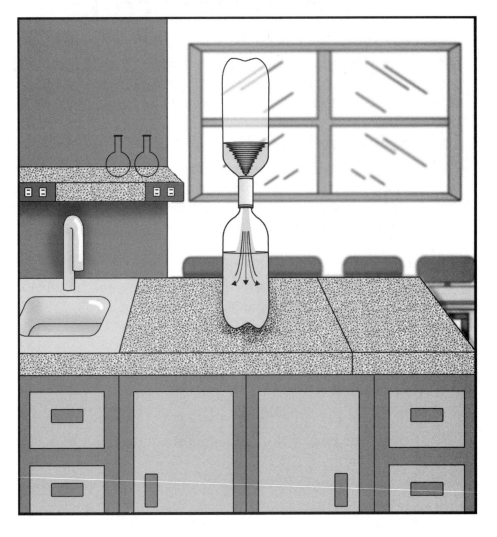

Describe Your Results

1. What did you observe in the bottle?

   _____

   _____

2. What happened when you rotated the bottle in the opposite direction?

   _____

   _____

Raining Frogs *(Continued)*

3. The spinning water is called a vortex. What does it look like?

_____

_____

What's the Solution?

Now that you have completed the lab, use what you discovered to solve "The Mystery of the Raining Frogs." Additional hints: A vortex can also be spinning air. A powerful vortex on land is called a tornado.

Exercises

Fill in the blanks with the correct answer:

1. Raining frogs have been seen in _____, England, and _____, Mexico.
2. A waterspout is like a _____.
3. Waterspouts can develop speeds of _____.
4. Spinning water or air is called a _____.

True or False?
1. In 1997, it rained frogs in Sineola, Mexico. _____
2. Waterspouts always occur over land. _____
3. Waterspouts are always huge. _____
4. The spinning water in the bottle is a vortex. _____

Unscramble these words from the activity:

1. DNWI _____
2. ODNRTOA _____
3. PTSUO _____
4. ESPRUSER _____
5. TVROXE _____

Extension

How is a hurricane different from a tornado or a waterspout?

12. The Mystery of the Glowing Ball of Light

In the summer of 1932, Victoria Mignotte Mondello was visiting her father's farm in Southwick, Massachusetts. A violent thunderstorm approached in the distance while Victoria was talking on the telephone. She was startled by a flash of lightning and looked out of the window. She saw a glowing ball of bright light rolling along the telephone line leading into the farmhouse. Victoria heard a loud crackling noise. Startled, she dropped the phone as a small ball of glowing light jumped out of the phone receiver, bounced several times on the floor and exited the farmhouse, blowing a hole in the screen door! Victoria was unharmed. She had just had an encounter with ball lightning. What is this strange phenomenon?

Lab: Let's Roll

Atoms are the smallest pieces of matter that keep the chemical properties of the element they make up. All atoms are made of electrons, which have a negative charge; protons, which have a positive charge; and neutrons, which have no charge. Static electricity is electricity created when atoms lose or gain electrons. In this lab, we will examine how static electricity is produced when some common objects are rubbed together.

Materials

Several pieces of Styrofoam packing peanuts

Balloon

Clear plastic drinking cup

What to Do

1. Blow up the balloon and tie it off.
2. Place several small broken pieces of Styrofoam into the clear plastic cup.
3. Turn the cup over on a flat surface.
4. Rub the balloon on your sleeve or on your hair. This is called charging the balloon.
5. Bring the balloon close to but not touching the clear plastic cup. Observe.
6. Bring the balloon close to and touch the cup before pulling the balloon away. Observe.

Glowing Ball of Light *(Continued)*

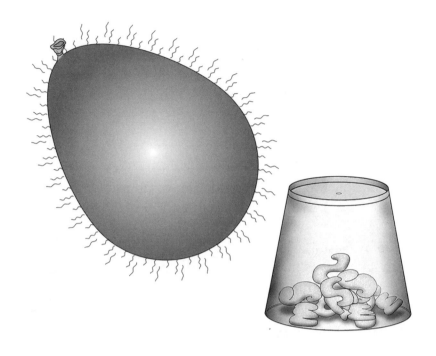

Describe Your Results

1. What did you see when you brought the balloon close to but not touching the plastic cup?

   _____

   _____

2. What did you see when you touched the plastic cup with the balloon?

   _____

   _____

What's the Solution?

Now that you have completed the lab, use what you discovered to solve "The Mystery of the Glowing Ball of Light." Additional hints: When you walk across a woolen rug and touch something metal you feel a shock, and if it's dark you may see a spark. If you ruffle your woolen blanket in the dark on a cold winter night, you might see sparks and hear a crackling noise. What do these things have in common with the lab and the mystery?

Glowing Ball of Light *(Continued)*

Exercises

Fill in the blanks with the correct answer:

1. Victoria's father lived on a _____ .
2. Victoria saw a phenomenon called _____ .
3. The ball of light blew a _____ in the screen door.
4. Atoms are made up of _____, protons, and neutrons.
5. Rubbing a balloon on your sleeve or your hair produces

   _____ .

True or False?

1. Victoria was not harmed by the ball lightning. _____
2. The ball lightning on Victoria's father's farm never entered the house. _____
3. Ball lightning doesn't occur during thunderstorms.

   _____

4. Protons have a positive charge and neutrons have a negative charge. _____

Unscramble these words from the activity:

1. CSATTI _____
2. GLGNITNIH _____
3. LLBA _____
4. PSRAK _____
5. NBOOALL _____

Extensions

1. Place very small pieces of paper into the upside down clear plastic cup and see what happens when you touch the cup with the charged balloon.
2. Try this in the dark in front of a mirror. Place a piece of wintergreen Life Saver candy in one side of your mouth between your back teeth. With your mouth open, break the Life Saver with your back teeth and watch what happens.

Copyright © 2006 by John Wiley & Sons, Inc.

13. The Mystery of the Green Flash

No, we're not talking about a superhero! The Green Flash is something you might see from Florida's west coast when the sun dips below the horizon on a hot summer's day. Just as the sun disappears below the water's edge, an odd green flash momentarily occurs and then it is gone! What causes this mysterious phenomenon?

Lab: Bubble, Bubble

Reflected light is something that bounces off something, while refracted light is light that is bent as it passes through something.

In this lab, we will examine what happens to light as it passes through a prism and through bubbles.

Materials

A prism (can be purchased from any science supply company)

Bubble solution and wand

Reflected Light

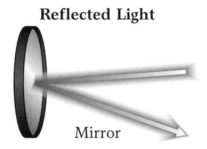

Mirror

Refracted Light (Bent)

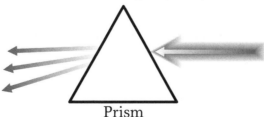

Prism

Green Flash *(Continued)*

What to Do

1. Place the prism in bright sunlight near a window.
2. Look around the room until you see a colored image that is projected from the prism. Observe it closely.
3. Use the bubble solution and wand to blow bubbles into the air.
4. Look closely at the bubbles as light passes through them.

Describe Your Results

1. What colors did you observed when the light went through the prism?

   _____

   _____

2. What was the total number of colors that you observed?

   _____

   _____

3. Write the first letter of each of the colors that you observe in order starting with R for red. <u>R</u> __ __ __ __ __

4. What colors did you observe passing through the bubbles?

   _____

   _____

What's the Solution?

Now that you have completed the lab, use what you discovered to solve "The Mystery of the Green Flash." Additional hints: A prism separates visible light into the colors of the spectrum: red, orange, yellow, green, blue, and violet. The bubble is made out of soap and water and acts as a prism. The Green Flash seems to only occur over bodies of water.

Green Flash *(Continued)*

Exercises

Fill in the blanks with the correct answer:

1. Light can be _____.
2. The colors that make up visible light are _____

   _____.

3. A _____ separates visible light into the colors of the spectrum.
4. The G stands for the color _____.

True or False?

1. When light passes through a prism it bends. _____
2. Bent light is reflected light. _____
3. The Green Flash only seems to occur over water.

   _____

4. The Green Flash lasts for about twenty minutes.

   _____

5. A prism refracts light. _____

Unscramble these words from the activity:

1. NGEER _____
2. TFARECR _____
3. DRE _____
4. RLTEFCE _____
5. SFHLA _____

Extension

Scratch several straight lines across a clear piece of overhead projector plastic. Look across these scratches in sunlight. Describe what you see.

14. The Mystery of Yellow Fever

Yellow fever is a tropical disease that occurs in parts of South America and Africa. People who catch the disease develop high fevers and can die. The name yellow fever comes from the yellow color its victims turn due to liver failure.

For a long time, no one understood how the disease was spread, although there were several theories. One was that the "bad night air" around swampy areas caused the disease. Another was that if you touched a person or came in contact with clothing or bed linen belonging to a person that had the disease, you would come down with yellow fever.

During the Spanish-American War of 1898, many more American soldiers died of yellow fever in Cuba than died in combat. The army imposed strict sanitation measures in Cuba, but outbreaks of fever continued to occur. In 1900 the army chose Major Walter Reed to head the Yellow Fever Commission to look into the matter. See if you can figure out how Major Reed solved "The Mystery of Yellow Fever."

Lab: The Cabin Experiment

In this lab, we'll examine Walter Reed's famous Cabin Experiment.

Materials

None

What to Do

Read the following:

In 1900, Walter Reed decided to test each theory by creating specific conditions in four cabins at an army camp in Cuba where yellow fever was known to occur.

Yellow Fever *(Continued)*

Cabin #1

Several volunteers slept with

    a. Windows closed

    b. Clean sheets

    c. Mosquito netting

Cabin #2

Several volunteers slept with

    a. Windows open

    b. Clean sheets

    c. Mosquito netting

Cabin #3

Several volunteers slept with

    a. Windows closed

    b. Sheets used by people who suffered from yellow fever

    c. Mosquito netting

Cabin #4

One volunteer slept with

    a. Windows closed

    b. Clean sheets

    c. Mosquito net with several mosquitoes under the netting (the volunteer was bitten several times)

Results: Only the volunteer in cabin #4 caught yellow fever. Miraculously he survived!

Describe Your Results

1. The Cabin Experiment was a controlled experiment. A controlled experiment has one thing varied in each test and a control, in which no variables are being tested. Which cabin exhibited the "perfect situation" (the control) in which no one should have contracted yellow fever?

The Mystery of Yellow Fever

Yellow Fever *(Continued)*

2. What was different in cabin #2? What do you think was being tested?

   _____

   _____

3. What was different in cabin #3? What do you think was being tested?

   _____

   _____

4. What was different in cabin #4? What do you think was being tested?

   _____

   _____

What's the Solution?

Now that you have completed the lab, use what you discovered to solve "The Mystery of Yellow Fever."

Exercises

Fill in the blanks with the correct answer:

1. Yellow fever is a _____ disease that occurs in parts of South America and Africa.
2. Yellow fever can cause _____ failure.
3. The man who discovered the cause of yellow fever was _____.
4. The famous Cabin Experiment was a _____ _____.

Yellow Fever *(Continued)*

True or False?

1. In the Spanish-American War, more soldiers died in combat in Cuba than died of yellow fever. _____

2. Walter Reed solved the mystery of yellow fever.

   _____

3. Cabin #4 tested the effects of mosquitoes. _____

4. The volunteer in cabin #4 died. _____

5. All the participants of the Cabin Experiment were volunteers.

   _____

Unscramble these words from the activity:

1. OTMSOQUI _____
2. VRFEE _____
3. ABUC _____
4. ANCBI _____
5. EEDR _____

Extension

The Panama Canal was built at the turn of the last century. How did Walter Reed's Cabin Experiment affect the successful completion of this project?

15. The Mystery of Greek Fire

Callinicus, a Syrian engineer who lived in the seventh century, is believed to have invented Greek Fire, a secret chemical mixture that burst into flames when it hit enemy ships. The mixture, which was shot from a long tube more than twelve hundred years before the invention of the cannon, was said to burn even under water. How was it possible to shoot this dangerous chemical over a long distance without a cannon?

Lab: Pow!

In this lab, we will examine what happens when two chemicals, vinegar and baking soda, are mixed in a container. What is the result of this chemical reaction?

Materials

Eyedropper

Small mount of liquid soap

One large 1-hole rubber stopper

Piece of tissue paper

Two tablespoons of baking soda (bicarbonate of soda)

One empty, clear 1-liter plastic bottle

150 ml of vinegar (acetic acid)

Glycerin

Elastic band

2-inch length of string

What to Do

1. Remove the rubber squeeze end of the eyedropper.
2. Put a little liquid soap on the smaller end of the eyedropper.
3. Slide the small end of the eyedropper through a large 1-hole rubber stopper to form a nozzle.
4. Place 2 tablespoons of baking soda into the tissue paper.
5. Fold the tissue securely around the baking soda to make a soft bag.
6. Place 150 ml of vinegar into the clear plastic 1-liter bottle.
7. Keeping the bottle upright, carefully squeeze the tissue pouch containing the baking soda into the mouth of the bottle, catching the tissue with the rubber stopper nozzle.

Greek Fire *(Continued)*

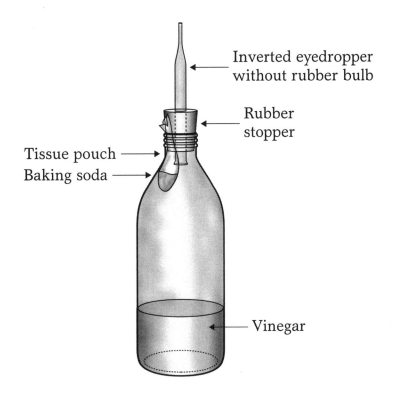

Inverted eyedropper without rubber bulb

Rubber stopper

Tissue pouch

Baking soda

Vinegar

8. Point the stoppered end of the bottle into a sink or take it outside. DO NOT POINT THE BOTTLE AT ANYONE.

Greek Fire (Continued)

9. Shake the bottle, keeping the top pointed away from yourself and anyone else. Observe.

Describe Your Results

1. What did you observe when you shook the bottle?

   _____

   _____

2. What are the chemical substances used in this lab activity?

   _____

   _____

3. What did the mixture produced by mixing the vinegar and baking soda look like?

   _____

   _____

4. How did the mixture leave the bottle?

   _____

   _____

What's the Solution?

Now that you have completed the lab, use what you discovered to solve "The Mystery of Greek Fire."

Exercises

Fill in the blanks with the correct answer.

1. _____ invented Greek Fire.
2. Greek Fire is reported to _____ even under water.
3. Greek Fire set _____ on fire.

Greek Fire *(Continued)*

4. Mixing vinegar and baking soda produces a _____
_____.

5. Vinegar and baking soda are _____.

True or False?

1. Greek Fire was used to cook food. _____

2. Greek Fire was shot from a cannon. _____

3. The recipe for Greek Fire was a secret. _____

4. Mixing chemicals together may produce chemical reactions.
_____

Unscramble these words from the activity:

1. RGEEK _____
2. EIRF _____
3. HMCAIECL _____
4. NONANC _____
5. HSPI _____

Extension

When vinegar and baking soda are mixed together, a gas is produced.
What is the name of this gas and how is this gas used in everyday life?

16. The Mystery of the Lindow Moss Bog Man

In the 1980s, a worker discovered a body in a peat bog at Lindow Moss, Cheshire, England. He called the police, who dug out the body and had it examined by scientists. As it turned out, the man had been murdered—about 2,000 years ago! The body was completely preserved, or mummified. Even the skin was intact. How was it possible for this body to remain in such good condition for such a long, long time?

Lab: Preservative

In this lab, we'll examine how an organic material can be preserved.

Materials

Two apple slices
Juice of one lemon or several drops of concentrated lemon juice
Two plastic or glass tumblers
Plastic wrap

What to Do

1. Rub lemon juice onto one apple slice.
2. Place this apple slice into one plastic or glass tumbler.
3. Place the other apple slice into the second tumbler.
4. Seal the mouth of both tumblers with plastic wrap.
5. Set the tumblers aside.
6. After one hour, observe both apple slices.
7. Wait another hour and again observe the apple slices.

Describe Your Results

1. What did the apple slices look like at the beginning of the experiment?

_____

2. What did the apple slices look like after one hour?

_____

Lindow Moss Bog Man *(Continued)*

3. What did the apple slices look like after two hours?

_____

What's the Solution?

Now that you have completed the lab, use what you discovered to solve "The Mystery of the Lindow Moss Bog Man." Additional hints: Bogs have a high acid content and low oxygen levels. Lemon juice is an acid.

Exercises

Fill in the blanks with the correct answer:

1. The Bog Man was found in a _____ in England.
2. The Bog Man is approximately _____ years old.
3. The Bog Man was completely preserved, or _____.
4. Peat bogs have a high _____ content.

True or False?

1. The Lindow Moss Bog Man was murdered. _____
2. The Bog Man is about 200 years old. _____
3. A preserved human body is called a mummy. _____
4. The Bog Man's skin had rotted away. _____

Unscramble these words from the activity:

1. OGB _____
2. MMMYU _____
3. INKS _____
4. DCAI _____
5. NDALGEN _____

Extension

pH is a scale that measures the acidity or alkalinity of a solution (ranks how acid or basic it is). A pH test kit can be purchased at most pet stores for testing fish tanks. Use one of these kits to test various liquids around the house. Write down the type of liquid tested and its pH.

17. The Mystery of the Vanished Cliff Dwellers

In the southwestern corner of Colorado there is a mountainous area called Mesa Verde. It was here in 1888 that two cowboys searching for lost cattle stopped at the edge of a canyon and saw below them a magnificent lost city! They had discovered an incredible city of cliff dwellings, in which the buildings were carved right out of the rock and into the sides of the mountains. The cliff dwellings were made by the Anasazi Indians around one thousand years ago. About a hundred years after building the city the Anasazi mysteriously disappeared, leaving their amazing rock-carved city vacant. Why did these people vanish?

Lab: Vanished!

In this lab, we'll examine water and an interesting chemical called sodium polyacrylate.

Although the disappearance of the Anasazi didn't have anything to do with this chemical, the surprising result of this experiment will give you a clue to one of the three reasons historians think the Anasazi may have disappeared.

Materials

Water

Two 8-ounce Styrofoam cups

Sodium polyacrylate (available from science supply companies)

Pencil

What to Do

1. Fill one of the Styrofoam cups with water.
2. Place 2 tablespoons of sodium polyacrylate into the other Styrofoam cup.
3. Pour the water into the cup containing the sodium polyacrylate. Observe.
4. Stab the pencil through the water and sodium polyacrylate cup. Turn the cup upside-down. Observe.

Vanished Cliff Dwellers *(Continued)*

Describe Your Results

1. What did the sodium polyacrylate look like before water was added to the cup?

   _____

   _____

2. What happened after the water was added to the cup?

   _____

   _____

3. What happened when the cup was turned upside-down?

   _____

   _____

What's the Solution?

Now that you have completed the lab, use what you discovered to solve "The Mystery of the Vanished Cliff Dwellers." Additional hint: Scientists think that unsanitary conditions and overcrowding were the two other possible reasons that the Anasazi disappeared.

Exercises

Fill in the blanks with the correct answer:

1. Mesa Verde is found in _____ .
2. The cliff dwellings were carved right out of the _____ .
3. The _____ lived at Mesa Verde.
4. The Cliff Dwellers _____ about a hundred years after building the city.

Vanished Cliff Dwellers *(Continued)*

True or False?

1. Two cowboys discovered Mesa Verde in the late 1800s.
   _____

2. The cliff dwellings were made out of wood. _____

3. The Anasazi lived in the cliff dwellings for 500 years.
   _____

4. Unsanitary conditions and overcrowding are two possible reasons
   for the disappearance of the Anasazi. _____

Unscramble these words from the activity:

1. IZNSAAA _____
2. LFCFI _____
3. DLLSREWE _____
4. ANUINTRYAS _____
5. PPSIDAAEERD _____

Extensions

1. What would be a good use for sodium polyacrylate in our everyday
   lives?

2. Add a couple of teaspoons of salt to the cup after the reaction is
   complete and describe what happens.

18. The Mystery of Bigfoot

In the vast forests of America's Northwest there have been many reported sightings of a mysterious hairy creature nicknamed Bigfoot for the extremely large footprints it leaves behind. This unknown creature has been described as being about six feet tall, walking upright on two legs, and having a large head and large feet, with hair covering its whole body. The Northwest Indians call this creature Sasquatch, and they say they have known of its existence for a long time. No one has ever gotten close to this strange creature, but some people claim to have captured it on film. How can we be certain whether this is a real creature or just someone running around in a monkey suit?

Lab: Match Game

In this lab, we'll examine how forensic scientists use DNA (deoxyribonucleic acid) to solve mysteries. DNA is a protein code found in the cells of living things. It is possible through a chemical process to take a picture of these proteins. Every living thing has its own unique DNA code and its own DNA picture.

Materials

DNA diagram set

What to Do

Here is a picture example of a DNA code.

Bigfoot (Continued)

Examine the following DNA picture sets. (Note: These are not actual DNA samples but have been fabricated especially for this lab. Each line of the basic DNA picture is always in exactly the same place for a particular living thing. For example, all cats have the same basic DNA picture.)

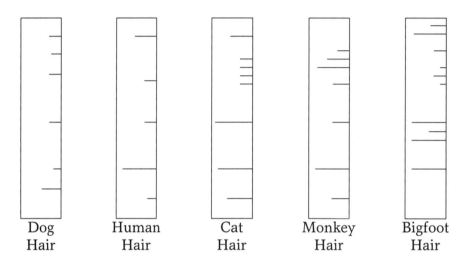

| Dog Hair | Human Hair | Cat Hair | Monkey Hair | Bigfoot Hair |

Describe Your Results

1. What does a DNA picture look like?

   _____

   _____

2. Is the dog hair DNA picture like the human DNA picture?

   _____

   _____

3. Is the cat hair DNA picture like the monkey DNA picture?

   _____

   _____

4. Do any of the DNA pictures match each other?

   _____

   _____

Bigfoot *(Continued)*

What's the Solution?

Now that you have completed the lab, use what you discovered to solve "The Mystery of Bigfoot." Additional hint: Hair samples from recent Bigfoot sighting locations have been tested by using forensic DNA identification techniques.

Exercises

Fill in the blanks with the correct answer:

1. Bigfoot sightings have occurred in the forests of the American
   _____ .

2. Bigfoot is said to have _____ covering its whole body.

3. The Indian name of Bigfoot is _____ .

4. No one has gotten close to _____ .

5. It is possible to take a _____ of DNA.

True or False?

1. Bigfoot was named for its large footprints. _____

2. Bigfoot has been described as being 10 feet tall.
   _____

3. DNA cannot be used to identify living things. _____

4. Every living thing has its own DNA code. _____

Unscramble these words from the activity:

1. NDA _____

2. ASSAUQHCT _____

3. RFSOENCI _____

4. RHIA _____

5. TOBOIGF _____

Extension

Draw a picture of what you think Bigfoot might look like.

19. The Mystery of Noah's Ark

According to those who have studied the Biblical story of Noah, Noah's Ark was supposed to have been approximately 450 feet long, 25 feet wide, and 50 feet tall, and completely built of wood. Scientists tell us that such a large ship built only of wood would break apart from its own weight. (Today we have ships that are even larger than this, but these ships are reinforced with steel.)

Could a wooden ship of that size have existed? See whether you can solve "The Mystery of Noah's Ark."

Lab: Boats Away!

In this lab, we'll examine a possible way that a huge ship could support its own weight.

Materials

Paper

Scissors

Pencil

Cellophane tape

Plastic bucket

Water

Paper clips

What to Do

1. Draw a square three inches on each side on a piece of white copy paper. Repeat this to make a total of four squares.

2. Draw a diagonal line from one corner to the opposite corner on one of the squares. Repeat this with the other corners. (See diagram.)

Noah's Ark *(Continued)*

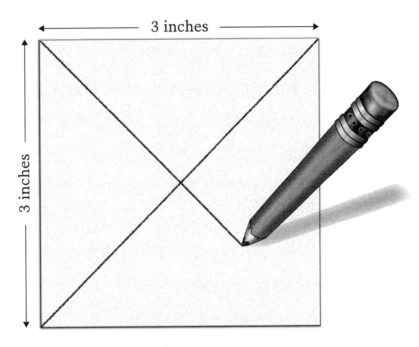

3. Repeat this for all squares.
4. Measure one-half inch in on each diagonal line and place a pencil mark.
5. Draw a line from pencil mark to pencil mark. (See diagram.)

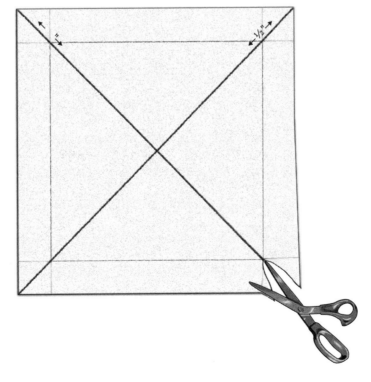

Noah's Ark *(Continued)*

6. Repeat on all squares.

7. Using scissors, cut in on each line just as far as the pencil mark on all four squares. Fold up the four edges of each square.

8. Using cellophane tape, fasten corners of one square to make a square paper tray.

9. Repeat this for all squares.

10. Place water into a bucket.

11. Float one paper square in the bucket of water.

12. Using cellophane tape, attach all four trays together to make one large tray with four compartments.

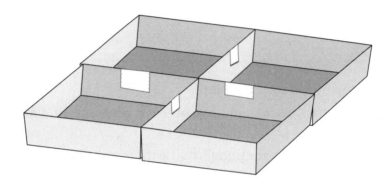

13. Float the large paper tray in the bucket of water.

14. Place two paper clips into each compartment. Observe.

Describe Your Results

1. What happened to one tray square when you put it in the water?

   _____

   _____

2. What happened to all the tray squares connected together in the water?

   _____

   _____

Noah's Ark *(Continued)*

3. What happened when you put paper clips in the compartments?

_____

_____

What's the Solution?

Now that you have completed the lab, use what you discovered to solve "The Mystery of Noah's Ark." Additional hint: Each paper tray represents a compartment in the larger ship.

Exercises

Fill in the blanks with the correct answer:

1. Noah's Ark was reportedly _____ feet long, _____ feet wide, and _____ feet tall.
2. The Ark was made of _____.
3. Modern ships are reinforced with _____.

True or False?

1. The story of Noah's Ark comes from the Bible.

   _____

2. Noah's Ark was made of steel. _____
3. Scientists say a wooden ark of this size would break apart.

   _____

Unscramble these words from the activity:

1. AHNO _____
2. PHSI _____
3. KRA _____
4. ELTES _____
5. TTMNEPRACOM _____

Extensions

1. Find out how many paper clips one square tray can hold before sinking.
2. Repeat with the four-compartment tray.

20. The Mystery of Napoleon's Death

In 1815, the French Emperor Napoleon was defeated at the Battle of Waterloo and was exiled to St. Helena, a tiny island in the middle of the South Atlantic Ocean. He lived there under British guard for six years, then passed away at the age of 52 under mysterious circumstances.

During the 1960s a lock of Napoleon's hair was examined by a team of forensic scientists and was found to contain a small amount of arsenic (a deadly poison).

Napoleon was ill when he arrived on the island. But did Napoleon's British jailers hasten his death by poisoning him?

Lab: Poisonous

In this lab, we'll examine three sets of data pertaining to the death of Napoleon. Arsenic is a yellowish mineral that is found in nature. In the past it has been used for rat poison, yellow paint pigment, and green paint pigment. Sometimes it was used to poison unfortunate victims over a long time because it was hard to detect. At one point arsenic was even known as the "inheritance poison." (Can you guess why?) Today forensic scientists can easily detect it by examining the blood and tissue of a suspected victim.

Materials

Data sets 1, 2, and 3

What to Do

Examine the following data sets:

Data Set 1: Common Places Arsenic Was Found

Glue

Yellow paint pigment

Green paint pigment

Rat poison

Pesticides

Contaminated water

Some medicines

Some plants

Pressure-treated wood

Napoleon's Death *(Continued)*

Cigarettes

Dietary supplements for children

Wine

Food

Crockery

Data Set 2: Napoleon's Surroundings on St. Helena

Tropical weather

Very humid house

Moldy odor in house

Billiard room with green-colored wallpaper that was peeling

Wine served with every meal

Data Set 3: Other Relevant Facts

Scientists discovered that a certain type of green wallpaper dye when exposed to damp conditions gave off arsenic vapors (gas).

During the last months of his life, Napoleon stayed inside all the time.

Napoleon's butler died soon after him.

Describe Your Results

1. What valuable clues are present in data set 1?

   _____

   _____

2. What valuable clues are present in data set 2?

   _____

   _____

3. Why is the information in data set 3 important?

   _____

   _____

Napoleon's Death *(Continued)*

What's the Solution?

Now that you have completed the lab, use what you discovered to solve "The Mystery of Napoleon's Death."

Exercises

Fill in the blanks with the correct answer:

1. Napoleon was exiled to _____.
2. Scientists found a small amount of _____ in Napoleon's hair.
3. Arsenic was used as poison because it was hard to _____.
4. Today, scientists can identify arsenic in a victim's _____ and _____.
5. Napoleon's _____ passed away soon after him.

True or False?

1. Arsenic is not a common poison. _____
2. The French guarded Napoleon on St. Helena. _____
3. Arsenic has been used in medicines. _____
4. During the last months of Napoleon's life, he stayed indoors. _____
5. St. Helena was cool and dry. _____

Unscramble these words from the activity:

1. ANPLONOE _____
2. CAERSNI _____
3. RAVPO _____
4. EENALH _____
5. DHIMU _____

Extension

Identify the characteristics of arsenic.

21. The Mystery of Lucy's Dinner

In 1974, a skeleton of a short, small-brained creature was found in the plains of Africa. Scientists determined that this creature was originally 3 to 4 feet tall, weighed approximately 65 pounds, and walked upright. The skeleton was dated at 3.5 million years old! The scientists who discovered the skeleton called it Lucy and identified it as an early ancestor to man. Lucy was found in an area where small tools were present but no obvious weapons. Some scientists believe that early humans were vegetarians or could have gotten their protein from legumes, small animals, and insects. Other scientists believe that Lucy and her relatives were more aggressive protein eaters. How could such a small hominid (ancestor of man) obtain protein from the large creatures of that period without the benefit of weapons?

Lab: Where's the Beef?

In this lab, we'll examine a protein source other than meat.

Materials

Dried chicken bone

Butter knife

Plastic cup

One cup water

Iron test material (can be ordered from science supply company)

What to Do

1. Take a dried chicken bone and on a clean flat surface use a butter knife to split it open.
2. Remove the sandy material (bone marrow) from the inside of the bone.
3. In a plastic cup, mix a small amount of the bone marrow with one cup of water.
4. Add the iron testing chemical to the water. This will indicate whether the material contains iron. (Protein is high in iron.) Observe.

Lucy's Dinner (Continued)

Describe Your Results

1. What color is the marrow from the chicken bone?

   _____

2. After the marrow was mixed with the iron testing chemical, what color did it turn?

   _____

3. What does the color change tell you about the bone marrow?

   _____

   _____

What's the Solution?

Now that you have completed the lab, use what you discovered to solve "The Mystery of Lucy's Dinner."

Exercises

Fill in the blanks with the correct answer:

1. Lucy is a skeleton that was _____ years old.
2. Lucy walked _____.
3. Lucy originally weighed about _____ pounds and was between _____ and _____ feet tall.
4. Protein is high in _____.
5. All humans need _____ to live.

True or False?
1. Lucy was found in South America. _____
2. Lucy was less than 3 feet tall. _____
3. Lucy was an ancestor of modern man. _____
4. Lucy was discovered in an area where small tools were present.
   _____
5. Iron is not contained in protein. _____

Lucy's Dinner *(Continued)*

Unscramble these words from the activity:

1. UYLC _____
2. LTOO _____
3. ONIR _____
4. NPTRIOE _____
5. ARMWOR _____

Extension

Who is Neanderthal man and when and where did he live?

22. The Mystery of the Burning Oak Tree

The lone oak tree stood in the midst of a group of maple and birch trees. In the distance, a thunderstorm gathered and steadily moved over the stand of trees. Rain poured down, drenching the trees and ground. Suddenly a blinding flash lit up the sky, thunder shook the ground, while a single bolt of lightning struck only the oak tree, splitting it in half and setting it on fire.

The mighty oak tree is struck by lightning more than any other type of tree, in fact, sixty times more than any other tree! What accounts for this mysterious phenomenon?

Lab: Zap!

In this lab, we'll examine the root growth of two different plants.

Materials

Two large tumblers or beakers

Water

Potato

Carrot

Toothpicks

What to Do

1. Fill each container with water.

2. Place at least four toothpicks around the potato, as pictured in the diagram.

3. Suspend the potato in the tumbler full of water, making sure that at least the bottom half of the potato is submerged in the water (see diagram).

Burning Oak Tree *(Continued)*

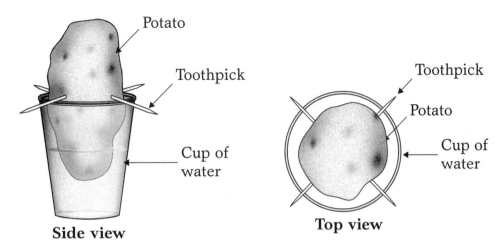

Side view

Top view

4. Place toothpicks around the whole carrot and arrange in a tumbler full of water in the same way as the potato.

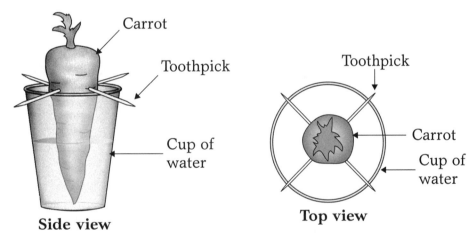

Side view

Top view

5. Set the two tumblers with suspended potato and carrot on a windowsill in full sunlight for several days.

6. Record your observations in the Data Chart.

Data Chart

	Day									
	1	**2**	**3**	**4**	**5**	**6**	**7**	**8**	**9**	**10**
Potato										
Carrot										

Burning Oak Tree *(Continued)*

7. Observe the diagrams of the following trees:

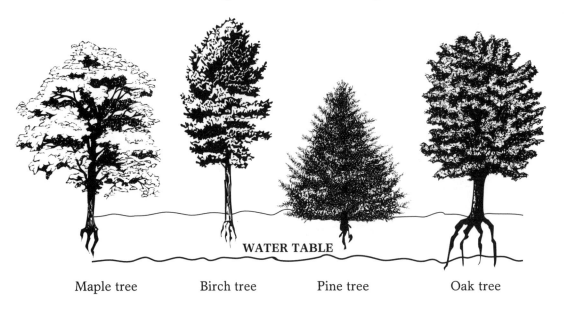

Maple tree   Birch tree   Pine tree   Oak tree

Describe Your Results

1. What happens to the potato and the carrot after a few days?

   _____

   _____

2. Which root system seemed to grow fastest?

   _____

3. Describe the root systems of the potato and the carrot.

   _____

   _____

4. Examine the pictures of the four trees. Describe the differences among their root systems.

   _____

   _____

5. Which of the four trees is connected to water?

   _____

Burning Oak Tree *(Continued)*

What's the Solution?

Now that you have completed the lab, use what you discovered to solve "The Mystery of the Burning Oak Tree." Additional hint: Water is an excellent conductor of electricity.

Exercises

Fill in the blanks with the correct answer:

1. The _____ is hit by lightning sixty times more than any other tree.
2. Water is an excellent conductor of _____.
3. The roots of the carrot are _____ .
4. The roots of the potato are _____ .
5. The roots of the oak tree reach the _____.

True or False?

1. Lightning will never seek out objects connected to water. _____
2. The water table is found on top of the ground. _____
3. The oak tree has a very deep root system. _____
4. Carrots and potatoes produce root systems. _____
5. Lightning cannot cause a tree to burn. _____

Unscramble these words from the activity:

1. ETRE _____
2. OTSRO _____
3. RETWA _____
4. GHITLIGNN _____
5. EBLAT _____

Extension

Repeat the lab with other vegetables, such as a radish, a sweet potato or yam, ginger, or a turnip.

23. The Mystery of the Oak Island Money Pit

Oak Island lies off the coast of Nova Scotia in Canada. According to legend, there is a valuable treasure contained in a cement vault 160 feet below the surface of the island. Over the years, people have dug a big pit in the ground in trying to get to the treasure. But every time treasure seekers dig into the pit, it fills up with water, preventing them from getting the treasure. Did someone who designed the pit figure out an ingenious trap to protect the treasure? Why does this pit fill with water every time an excavation is attempted? Let us solve "The Mystery of the Oak Island Money Pit."

Lab: Where Is the Leak?

In this lab, we'll examine how a siphon works.

air pressure

Materials

Two beakers (or plastic tumblers)   Water

Eyedropper   Five textbooks

3-foot length of latex tubing

What to Do

1. Fill a plastic tumbler (or beaker) three-fourths full of water.

2. Place the container on a table.

3. Using an eyedropper, place several drops of water into the latex tubing.

4. Cover both ends of the latex tubing with the index fingers of both hands.

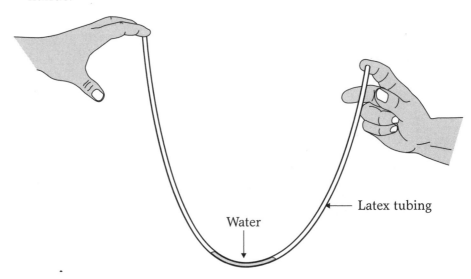

Water

Latex tubing

Oak Island Money Pit *(Continued)*

5. Place one end of the latex tubing at the bottom of the container with water. Remove your finger from this end.

6. While holding the latex tube in position in the beaker of water, place the other empty container on the floor.

7. Place the free end of the latex tubing into the empty container and remove your finger. Observe.

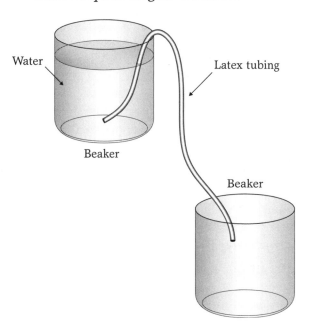

Water

Latex tubing

Beaker

Beaker

8. Look at the diagram of the Oak Island Money Pit.

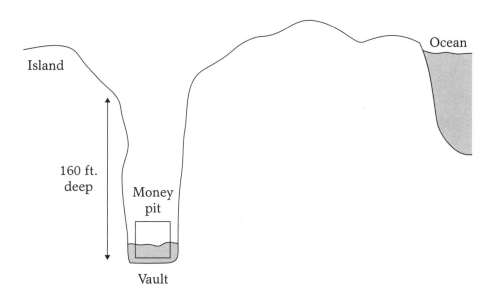

Island

Ocean

160 ft. deep

Money pit

Vault

Oak Island Money Pit *(Continued)*

9. Compare the diagram to your tubing and tumbler setup.
10. Repeat the activity, but instead of placing the second empty container on the floor, set it higher than the first container, on top of the five textbooks.

Describe Your Results

1. What happened when you put the tubing in the empty container and removed your finger?

   _____

   _____

2. What happened in the second trial, when you didn't put water in the tubing?

   _____

   _____

3. What happened in the third trial, when the second container was higher than the first?

   _____

   _____

4. Which trial was most effective in moving the water and why?

   _____

   _____

What's the Solution?

Now that you have completed the lab, use what you discovered to solve "The Mystery of the Oak Island Money Pit." Additional hints: Water runs downhill because of gravity. Pressure helps to push and pull water.

Oak Island Money Pit *(Continued)*

Exercises

Fill in the blanks with the correct answer:

1. Oak Island is located off the coast of _____ in Canada.
2. The Money Pit may hide a valuable _____.
3. Every time treasure hunters excavate the Pit, it fills up with _____.
4. Water runs _____ because of gravity.
5. The ocean around Oak Island is _____ than the Money Pit.

True or False?

1. The treasure is thought to be in a cement vault. _____
2. The vault is supposed to be 100 feet down in the pit.

   _____
3. All attempts to retrieve the treasure have failed. _____
4. Gravity is not involved in pulling water down the tubing.

   _____

Unscramble these words from the activity:

1. ETAERSUR _____
2. TPI _____
3. KAO _____
4. OSPNHI _____
5. OYENM _____

Extension

Repeat the activity, but replace the latex tubing with a length of twisted dry paper towel. Repeat it again with a length of twisted wet paper towel.

24. The Mystery of the Black Death

The Black Death is the common name for the bubonic plague that killed about one-third of the population of Europe around 1350 A.D. The symptoms of this disease were quite horrible, with the victims having very high fevers and spitting up blood. One form of the plague was so bad that victims usually died the same day symptoms appeared. In some cities, as many as 800 people died every day. Some people thought that the infection was spread by coming in contact with someone who had the disease or their clothes or bed linens. However, isolating the sick and burning their belongings did not seem to stop the plague. As the Black Death swept through Europe and each remedy failed, people thought the large cat populations in the cities were causing the disease. But when people started destroying all the cats, even more people got the plague! What was the mysterious cause of this horrible disease?

Lab: The Black Death

A predator–prey relationship is between the hunter and the hunted. An example of a predator–prey relationship is a hawk and a field mouse. The hawk is the hunter that eats or preys on the field mouse. Our environment has countless predator–prey relationships. If the balance between predators and prey is disturbed, it can affect the whole population of a species. In this lab, we'll take a look at some predator–prey relationships.

Materials

Predator–prey sheet

Scissors

Cellophane tape

Sheet of copy paper

What to Do

1. Use scissors to cut out each of the animals on the predator–prey sheet.

2. Match up the predator with its prey by taping them side by side on a sheet of copy paper.

Predator–Prey Sheet

Minnow

Deer

Owl

Rabbit

Field Mouse

Fly

Big Fish

Mountain Lion

Rat

Cat

Frog

Fox

Black Death (Continued)

Describe Your Results

1. What is the prey of the owl? _____
2. What is the predator of the deer? _____
3. What is the prey of the fox? _____
4. What is the predator of the rat? _____
5. What is the predator of the minnow? _____
6. What is the prey of the frog? _____
7. Which predator and its prey would be most likely to be found in cities? _____

What's the Solution?

Now that you have completed your lab, use what you discovered to solve "The Mystery of the Black Death." Additional hint: What animal population would have increased if the people killed off all the cats?

Exercises

Fill in the blanks with the correct answer:

1. About _____ of the population of Europe was killed by the Black Death.
2. The Black Death is also called the _____.
3. Some people thought that _____ were spreading the disease.
4. A predator is a _____.
5. A prey is the _____.

Black Death *(Continued)*

True or False?

1. The predator of the rabbit is the fox. _____

2. The prey of the cat is the rat. _____

3. Victims of the Black Death had very high fevers. _____

4. Predator–prey relationships are rarely found in our environment.
_____

5. When the cats of the European cities were eliminated, the plague got worse. _____

Unscramble these words from the activity:

1. SRTA _____

2. CBALK EHTAD _____

3. YPER _____

4. TDREPROA _____

5. UEPALG _____

Extension

Make food chains from the following list of predators and prey:

Hawk, frog, snake, grass, insect,

Man, algae, small fish, tuna, shrimp

25. The Mystery of Galloping Gertie

The Tacoma Narrows Bridge that spanned Puget Sound in the state of Washington was nicknamed "Galloping Gertie" because it continually experienced a rocking and rolling motion, even during a light wind. People in cars driving on the bridge had the sensation of being on a roller coaster as vehicles traveling ahead of them would rise and then dip out of sight. This suspension bridge was designed to be the essence of grace and flexibility. It even had the shape of an airplane wing. The bridge was completed on July 1, 1940 and collapsed just four months later in wind of about 40 miles per hour, even though it had supposedly been designed to withstand winds of up to 120 miles per hour. Why did this bridge, which was considered state of the art for its time, collapse? See if you can solve "The Mystery of Galloping Gertie"!

Lab: Up and Away!

In this lab, we'll examine how the air pressure of moving air can vary and how that difference in air pressure affects objects that the air is moving around.

Materials

> Three pieces of copy paper
>
> A plastic or glass funnel
>
> A ping-pong ball

What to Do

1. Hold a sheet of copy paper below your lips and blow over the top (see diagram). Observe.

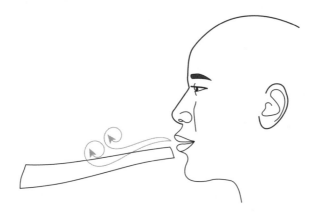

Galloping Gertie *(Continued)*

2. Hold two sheets of copy paper about one-half inch apart and blow down through the middle of the two sheets (see diagram). Observe.

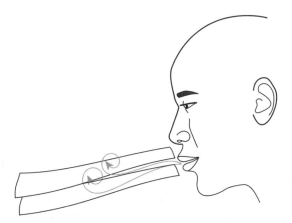

3. Place a ping-pong ball into a plastic funnel. Hold the ping-pong ball in place with your finger while pointing the larger end of the funnel toward the floor. Blow into the funnel forcefully and at the same time remove your finger from the ping-pong ball (see diagram). Observe.

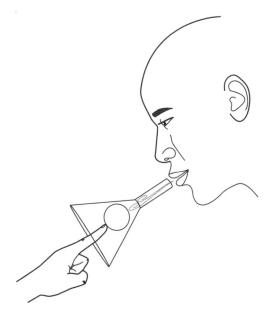

Describe Your Results

1. What happened in step 1 of the activity?

_____

_____

Galloping Gertie *(Continued)*

2. What happened in step 2 of the activity?

_____

_____

3. What happened in step 3 of the activity?

_____

_____

4. The diagram below shows a side view of an airplane wing, an airfoil. The air rushing over the top and bottom of the wing reaches the back end of the wing at the same time. This means that the air on top of the wing has to travel a longer distance so it must travel faster. The faster air has lower pressure than the slower air. How does this relate to what happened in the lab?

_____

_____

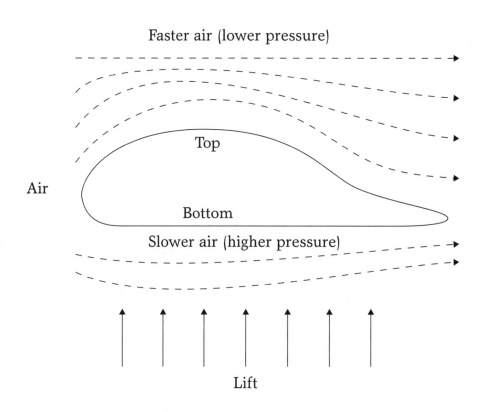

Faster air (lower pressure)

Top

Air

Bottom

Slower air (higher pressure)

Lift

Galloping Gertie *(Continued)*

What's the Solution?

Now that you have completed the lab, use what you learned to solve "The Mystery of Galloping Gertie." Additional hint: Higher pressure air pushes against lower pressure air.

Exercises

Fill in the blanks with the correct answer:

1. "Galloping Gertie" is the nickname for the _____
   _____.

2. The bridge was shaped like an _____.

3. The bridge _____ and rolled even in a light wind.

4. Four months after the bridge was completed, it _____.

5. The faster air traveling over an airplane wing has _____ pressure than the air traveling under the wing.

True or False?

1. The Tacoma Narrows Bridge lasted for four years. _____

2. Galloping Gertie only moved in very high winds. _____

3. The pressure on top of a wing is low while the pressure on the bottom of the wing is high. _____

4. This pressure difference causes lift for the airplane. _____

5. Blowing over a piece of paper causes lift. _____

Unscramble these words from the activity:

1. IETGRE _____
2. IGHH _____
3. ERSSERPU _____
4. DWNI _____
5. MOCTAA _____

Extension

In Boston there is a skyscraper called the John Hancock Tower that is entirely covered in glass. When the tower was nearly finished, the huge windows of this building began popping out and crashing to the streets below. Fortunately no one was seriously hurt. The tower's heavy energy-efficient windows sealed the building very tightly. Can you find out why they were popping out?

26. The Mystery of the Oregon Vortex

The Oregon Vortex is located at Gold Hill, Oregon. This area became known as the Vortex because human senses seem to spin out of control there. (A vortex is spinning air or water.) Native American tribes of the region call this area the Forbidden Ground. According to legend, Native American ponies would not walk within the boundaries of this region.

Strange sights greet you at the Vortex. People seem to change in height. Everything appears slanted the wrong way. Balls even seem to roll uphill. What causes these strange occurrences?

Lab: Seeing Is Believing

In this lab, we'll examine how perspective (how a person sees differences in distance and position) can dramatically change what we think we see.

Materials

Pencil

Sheet of copy paper

Ruler

What to Do

Activity 1

1. Cover one eye and look at any object.

2. Now repeat with the other eye.

3. Observe the differences.

Activity 2

1. Place the sheet of copy paper horizontally on a flat surface and, using a pencil and ruler, draw an 8-inch line on one side of the paper. Repeat on the other side of the paper. Draw two arrow points on each side of the line on the left. Reverse the arrow points on the right-hand line (see diagram).

Oregon Vortex *(Continued)*

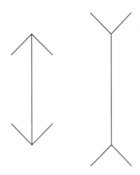

2. Examine each drawing. Do the lines still look like they are the same length?

Activity 3

Place the tips of the index fingers of your hands together and hold them a foot in front of your eyes. Slowly bring them closer to your eyes as you look at them. What happens?

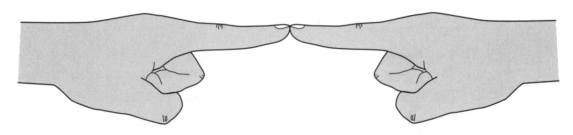

Describe Your Results

1. What did you see with each eye in Activity 1?

   _____

   _____

2. What happened to the way the two lines looked when the arrow points were added in Activity 2?

   _____

   _____

3. What happened in Activity 3 when you brought your fingers close to your eyes?

   _____

   _____

The Mystery of the Oregon Vortex   **85**

Oregon Vortex *(Continued)*

What's the Solution?

Now that you have completed the lab, use what you discovered to solve "The Mystery of the Oregon Vortex." Additional hint: Optical illusions are visual phenomena that are deceptive or misleading, or tricks of the eye.

Exercises

Fill in the blanks with the correct answer:

1. The Vortex is located in _____.
2. The Native Americans called the Vortex _____ _____.
3. Even Native American _____ would not walk into the Vortex.
4. The way you see differences in distance and position is called _____.
5. _____ illusions trick the eye.

True or False?
1. There is no such thing as an optical illusion. _____
2. The Vortex seems to confuse the senses. _____
3. People seem to change in height in the Vortex. _____
4. Perspective involves how we see things. _____
5. Position is not important to perspective. _____

Unscramble these words from the activity:

1. AILTPOC _____
2. INUSLIOL _____
3. EVITCEPSREP _____
4. XVTROE _____
5. GNEROO _____

Extension

You can examine a natural optical illusion the next time you see the large "Harvest Moon" in the night sky close to the horizon. Hold a ruler up to the sky and measure the width of the moon. After the moon has risen into the sky, it will appear to be much smaller. Measure its width again. What have you discovered?

27. The Mystery of the Taos Hum

Taos, New Mexico, is located in a very hot and dry region of the United States. Some inhabitants of the area complain of a continuous low-pitched noise that sounds like something made by a machine. Most people do not hear the noise, but enough of the population is affected that this strange occurrence has been given a name: The Taos Hum.

Some people say the hum makes them irritable, some experience headaches, and some say they have trouble sleeping. Can you solve "The Mystery of the Taos Hum"?

Lab: Craackk!!!

A fault is a crack or crevice in the earth's crust that can travel for hundreds of miles. The sections of the earth's crust on either side of the fault can move in three directions (see diagrams).

The two sides can move apart.

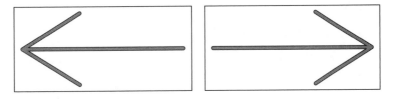

The two sides can move together.

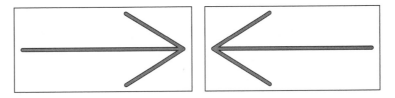

The two sides can slide past each other.

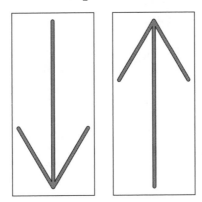

Taos Hum *(Continued)*

In this lab, we'll examine what happens when dry dirt particles are rubbed together.

Materials

Two pieces of copy paper

Eyedropper

Plastic cup with small amount of dirt

Plastic cup with small amount of water

What to Do

1. Place a piece of copy paper on a flat surface.
2. Sprinkle a small amount of dirt in the center of the paper.
3. Place the other piece of copy paper on top of the paper with the dirt.
4. Slide the top sheet slowly back and forth. Observe.
5. Remove the top sheet and add a few drops of water to the dirt.
6. Replace the top sheet and slide gently back and forth. Observe.

Describe Your Results

1. What happened when you rubbed the top sheet of paper over the dry dirt?

   _____

   _____

2. What happened after water was added to the dirt?

   _____

   _____

What's the Solution?

Now that you have completed the lab, use what you discovered to solve "The Mystery of the Taos Hum." Additional hints: Taos sits on a large fault or crack in the earth's crust. Taos, News Mexico, is in a very hot and dry area of the United States.

Taos Hum *(Continued)*

Exercises

Fill in the blanks with the correct answer:

1. The Taos Hum is a _____ noise.
2. Some people say the hum makes them have trouble

   _____.

3. Taos, New Mexico, is very hot and _____.
4. A fault is a _____ in the earth's crust.

True or False?

1. The Taos Hum is described as a machine-like noise.

   _____

2. The hum never gives anyone a headache. _____
3. Faults can move in five directions. _____
4. A fault can be hundreds of miles in length. _____

Unscramble these words from the activity:

1. NEOSI _____
2. STOA _____
3. OSCUOITNNU _____
4. YDR _____
5. TCURS _____

Extension

Try rubbing different substances, such as sugar, salt, baking soda, baking powder, flour, and cornstarch, between two sheets of paper. Which makes the most noise?

28. The Mystery of Cooking Without Heat

When we think of cooking we always think of a flame or a heated oven. Yet there are many cultures throughout history that have cooked food, including fish and even meat, without any type of flame or other heat. One benefit of this type of cooking is that it saves energy. How is it possible to cook without any heat or flame?

Lab: Cooking Cukes

In this lab, we'll examine a process that changes the taste and texture of a cucumber.

Materials

One small cucumber

Large plastic bowl with a tight-fitting cover

One quart of water

Four ounces of white vinegar

One tablespoon of salt

Three to four sprigs of dill

One teaspoon of peppercorns

What to Do

1. Wash the cucumber. Let it soak in water overnight.
2. Place the cucumber in the plastic container with the water.
3. Add the dill and peppercorns.
4. Add the vinegar and salt to the container.
5. Place the lid on the container and keep the container in the refrigerator for a week.
6. Observe at the end of the week (including taste).

Cooking Without Heat *(Continued)*

Describe Your Results

1. How does the cucumber look at the end of the week?

   _____

   _____

2. How does the cucumber feel (texture)?

   _____

   _____

3. How does the cucumber smell (odor)?

   _____

   _____

4. How does the cucumber taste?

   _____

   _____

5. What do you think happened to the cucumber?

   _____

   _____

What's the Solution?

Now that you have completed the lab, use what you discovered to solve "The Mystery of Cooking Without Heat." Additional hints: Vinegar is acetic acid. Water is composed of hydrogen and oxygen. Salt is sodium chloride. These chemicals can be part of a chemical reaction.

Cooking Without Heat *(Continued)*

Exercises

Fill in the blanks with the correct answer:

1. Many _____ have developed methods of cooking without heat.
2. Cooking _____ is a different method for preparing food.
3. Using no flame to cook saves _____.
4. The chemical name for vinegar is _____.

True or False?

1. The process of cooking without heat is hundreds of years old.
   _____
2. Fish could never be cooked without heat. _____
3. The chemical name for salt is calcium chloride. _____
4. Vinegar is an acid. _____

Unscramble these words from the activity:

1. TEAH _____
2. ATSL _____
3. KCOIOGN _____
4. GRAVNIE _____
5. BREMUCCU _____

Extension

Try "cooking" another fruit or vegetable, such as a tomato or a carrot, using the same method. Let it sit for several days. Observe the texture, appearance, and the taste.

29. The Mystery of Spontaneous Human Combustion

For hundreds of years people have reported cases of what's been called Spontaneous Human Combustion. In this phenomenon a human body seems to have suddenly burned without any outside source of ignition and with no damage to the area surrounding the victim.

In 1951, for example, Mary Reeser, age 67, was discovered in her apartment in Florida almost completely reduced to a pile of ashes. The only thing left of this unfortunate victim was a skull and an unburned left foot. There was a black circle around her chair, and nothing else in the apartment had been burned. No one has proven that spontaneous combustion is actually what killed Mary or anyone else. Could it be possible?

Lab: Whoosh! (Teacher Demonstration)

In this lab, we'll examine what happens when a tiny amount of water is placed on hot wax. We will also observe the effects of burning ethanol. Ethanol is alcohol that is made from fermented grains or fruits.

Materials

Porcelain evaporating dish

Eyedropper

1 ml of ethanol

Candle with candleholder

Plastic cup with a small amount of water

Safety goggles

Safety matches

What to Do

1. Set the candle in the candleholder. Carefully light the candle.
2. Observe the candle wax around the flame.
3. Wearing safety goggles, carefully place one drop of water into the liquid wax around the base of the burning candle wax. Observe.
4. Still wearing safety goggles, place several drops of ethanol into the porcelain-evaporating dish. Carefully ignite the ethanol with a safety match. Observe.

Spontaneous Human Combustion *(Continued)*

Describe Your Results

1. What did you observe when the few drops of water fell on the burning candle wax?

   _____

   _____

2. What is it that burns on a candle?

   _____

   _____

3. What color was the candle flame?

   _____

   _____

4. What happened when the ethanol was ignited?

   _____

   _____

5. What color was the ethanol's flame?

   _____

   _____

6. What can you say about both wax and ethanol?

   _____

   _____

What's the Solution?

Now that you have completed the lab, use what you have discovered to solve "The Mystery of Spontaneous Human Combustion." Additional hints: Wax is similar to fat, which is found in the human body. Ethanol is the main ingredient of alcoholic beverages, such as whiskey, wine, and beer.

Spontaneous Human Combustion *(Continued)*

Exercises

Fill in the blanks with the correct answer:

1. Spontaneous combustion happens without any outside source of

   _____.

2. Mary Reeser was almost completely reduced to a pile of

   _____.

3. Ethanol is _____ and is flammable.

4. Ethanol is made of fermented grains or _____.

5. Alcohol _____ with a blue flame.

True or false?

1. Mary Reeser died in 1981. _____
2. Candle wax and fat are not flammable. _____
3. Fat is found in the human body. _____
4. Wine and beer are made of ethanol. _____

Unscramble these words from the activity:

1. EBAAMMLLF _____
2. CLOOALH _____
3. SNAPTSOUONE _____
4. NBRU _____
5. MCOSUBTNOI _____

Extension

Why should you never throw water on burning fat or any type of liquid fire?

30. The Mystery of the Long Island Typhoid Outbreak

In late 1906, there was an outbreak of typhoid fever on Long Island in the state of New York. Typhoid is spread through water or foodstuffs and can be deadly. The Long Island Health Department investigated but found no contaminated water or food that would have caused this particular outbreak of typhoid. So how was it spread?

Lab 1: Germy

In this lab, we will examine how disease can be transmitted.

Study the following data comparing four households on Long Island at the time of the outbreak:

Set 1

Home 1: Eight people (no typhoid)

Jack T (father)	Flora T (mother)
James T (son)	Mike T (son)
Cara T (daughter)	John W (gardener)
Mavis A (cook)	Jane Z (maid)

Home 2: Eight people (two cases of typhoid)

Patrick S (father)	Margaret S (mother)
Jonathan S (son)	Fred S (son)
JoAnn S (daughter)	Gus B (gardener)
Mary M (cook)	Henry C (butler)

Home 3: Seven people (no typhoid)

Phil A (father)	Nancy A (mother)
Patricia A (daughter)	Maria A (daughter)
John E (gardener)	Roberta T (cook)
Alice F (maid)	

Home 4: Seven people (six cases of typhoid)

Richard M (father)	Elisha M (mother)
Kathleen M (daughter)	Jennifer M (daughter)
Caleb N (gardener)	Mary M (cook)
Ivonne O (maid)	

Long Island Typhoid Outbreak *(Continued)*

Set 2

People in the Home Over a Period of Eight Months

Home 1:   Jack T (father)   Flora T (mother)
            James T (son)   Mike T (son)
            Cara T (daughter)   John W (gardener)
            Mavis A (cook)   Jane Z (maid)

Home 2:   Patrick S (father)   Margaret S (mother)
            Jonathan S (son)   Fred S (son)
            JoAnn S (daughter)   Gus B (gardener)
            Mary M (cook)   Henry C (butler)

Home 3:   Phil A (father)   Nancy A (mother)
            Patricia A (daughter)   Maria A (daughter)
            John E (gardener)   Roberta T (cook)
            Alice F (maid)

Home 4:   Richard M (father)   Elisha M (mother)
            Kathleen M (daughter)   Jennifer M (daughter)
            Caleb N (gardener)   Mary M (cook)
            Ivonne O (maid)

Lab 2: Go Glow!

Materials

Glo Germ kit (This kit or a similar kit can be purchased from many
    science supply companies. It is a completely safe powder or lotion.
    The material is fluorescent, so it glows in ultraviolet light.)

Soap and water

Ultraviolet light

What to Do

1. Apply "germ" material from the kit to your hands.
2. Place your hands under the ultraviolet light. Observe.
3. Wash off the "germ" material completely with soap and water.
4. Place your hands under the ultraviolet light. Observe.

Long Island Typhoid
Outbreak *(Continued)*

Describe Your Results

1. In which homes in Lab 1 did people contract typhoid fever?

   _____

   _____

2. What similarities existed in the homes with typhoid?

   _____

   _____

3. What happened when you first placed your unwashed hands under the ultraviolet light?

   _____

   _____

4. What happened after you washed your hands and placed them under the ultraviolet light?

   _____

   _____

5. Consider the lab results: Why is it important that you wash your hands thoroughly before touching your food or your face?

   _____

   _____

What's the Solution?

Now that you have completed the lab, use what you discovered to solve "The Mystery of the Long Island Typhoid Outbreak."

Long Island Typhoid
Outbreak *(Continued)*

Exercises

Fill in the blanks with the correct answer:

1. The _____ Health Department
   was called in to investigate the outbreak of typhoid fever described
   in this activity.
2. The food and water they tested was not _____.
3. _____ materials glow in ultraviolet light.
4. An _____ light illuminated the germs.

True or False?

1. Typhoid fever is never fatal. _____
2. There were cases of typhoid found in three of the homes that you
   studied in the lab. _____
3. Germs glow in the dark. _____
4. Washing your hands gets rid of most germs. _____

Unscramble these words from the activity:

1. EGMR _____
2. HTPIDOY _____
3. TOURBAKE _____
4. GNWSAHI _____
5. EDAESIS _____

Extension

Find out what other diseases are spread by foods.

31. The Mystery of the Celt

At Stonehenge in England and at other ancient rock circles in the British Isles, archaeologists have dug up ancient stone adzes (a tool for gouging wood) and axes that date back 1,500 years and more. The axes are wedge shaped and the adzes are teardrop shaped but flat on one side. Scientists call these ancient tools "celts" (seltz). These ancient tools have a very mysterious property. See what this property is by following the steps in the lab below. Then see whether you can solve "The Mystery of the Celt."

Lab: Rock the House!

In this lab, we'll examine what happens when you spin an object with an ellipsoid (a three-dimensional oval shape) bottom.

Materials

A celt (inexpensive plastic celts can be purchased from many scientific supply houses)

What to Do

1. Examine the celt closely, noticing its shape.
2. Place the celt on a flat surface and spin it clockwise. Wait for it to come to a complete stop, then observe what happens.
3. Tap one end of the celt and observe what happens.

Describe Your Results

1. What did you notice about the celt's shape?

   _____

   _____

2. What happened when you spun the celt clockwise?

   _____

   _____

3. What happened when you tapped one end of the celt?

   _____

   _____

Celt *(Continued)*

What's the Solution?

Now that you have completed the lab, use what you discovered to solve "The Mystery of the Celt."

Exercises

Fill in the blanks with the correct answer:

1. Celts were ancient _____ called adzes.
2. Adzes were used to _____.
3. Stone adzes and axes date back _____ years and more.
4. The adzes are teardrop shaped, but _____ on one side.

True or False?

1. Archaeologists have discovered ancient stone adzes and axes at places like Stonehenge. _____
2. A celt only spins clockwise. _____
3. The celt has a rhomboid-shaped bottom. _____
4. The celt spins backwards before it rocks up and down.

   _____

Unscramble these words from the activity:

1. PTA _____
2. LCTE _____
3. KCRO _____
4. EAZD _____
5. NPSI _____

Extension

Celts are also called "rattlebacks" and "wobblestones." Find out more about these stones and the physics behind their strange spin.

32. The Mystery of the Hot Springs

Hot Springs, Arkansas, is the site of a natural wonder. There are a total of forty-seven springs in the area, which produce water at a temperature of about 143 degrees Fahrenheit.

Scientists tell us that the water gushing from the hot springs is around 4,000 years old. It actually took that length of time to trickle down through cracks and crevices to penetrate deeply into the earth's crust. This same water travels to the surface in less than a year to form the Hot Springs!

How is it possible for water to travel so quickly to the surface when it took so long to reach the depths of the earth? Let us solve "The Mystery of the Hot Springs."

Lab: Hot! Hot! Hot!

In this lab, we'll examine the effects of heat on a fluid. (Note: liquids and gases are both fluids.)

Materials

Balloon

Water

Dry sponge

What to Do

Activity 1

1. Blow up the balloon and tie it off.
2. Place the balloon somewhere cold, such as in the refrigerator. Observe.
3. Now place the balloon somewhere warm. Observe.

Activity 2

1. Pour a small puddle of water on a flat surface.
2. Place a dry sponge on the water. Observe.
3. When water has been completely absorbed, quickly squeeze the sponge very hard.

Hot Springs *(Continued)*

Describe Your Results

1. In Activity 1, what happens to the balloon in the refrigerator?

   _____

   _____

2. What happens when the balloon warms up again?

   _____

   _____

3. In Activity 2, how long does it take for the water to completely soak into the sponge?

   _____

   _____

4. What happens to the water when the sponge is squeezed quickly?

   _____

   _____

What's the Solution?

Now that you have completed the lab, use what you discovered to solve "The Mystery of the Hot Springs." Additional hint: The temperature inside the earth increases the deeper you go.

Exercises

Fill in the blanks with the correct answer:

1. Hot Springs is located in _____.
2. The water of the Hot Springs reaches a temperature of around _____.
3. It took the water about _____ to reach the depths of the earth.
4. The water reaches the surface in _____.

Hot Springs *(Continued)*

True or False?

1. There are forty-seven springs at Hot Springs, Arkansas.

   _____

2. The temperature deep in the earth is quite hot.

   _____

3. The balloon in the refrigerator shrunk in size (contracted).

   _____

4. The deeper you go into the earth, the hotter it gets.

   _____

Unscramble these words from the activity:

1. THO _____
2. DLCO _____
3. SSANARAK _____
4. GPINSR _____
5. RTWAE _____

Extension

Have you noticed that many highway bridges have metal strips running across the road? What do you think is the purpose of these long pieces of metal?

33. The Mystery of Easter Island

In 1722, a Dutch explorer, Jacob Roggeveen, discovered a strange island in the Pacific Ocean. The island, which is located 2,300 miles west of Chile, is triangular in shape and approximately 63 square miles in area. It rises sharply out of the sea, and was formed by three volcanoes.

What Roggeveen discovered on the island amazed him: more than 600 carved stone heads, some weighing as much as several tons and ranging in height from 12 feet to 25 feet. The civilization that carved the heads was gone by the time Roggeveen landed there.

The tallest of the Easter Island statues is unfinished. Its back is still part of a wall of volcanic rock from which it was being carved. But most of the heads are free standing and were somehow carried to their current positions. How could these huge prehistoric statues have been moved and set into place without modern-day equipment, such as cranes?

Lab: Ooof!

In this lab, we'll examine how work is made easier by using simple machines.

Materials

Sheet of newspaper

Textbook

Five wooden pencils

What to Do

1. Open the newspaper and spread it on top of a flat work surface. Place the textbook in the center of the sheet of newspaper.

2. Place your hand on top of the book and push it slowly across the flat work surface. Observe.

3. Again, place the textbook in the center of the newspaper.

4. Grip the edge of the newspaper nearest you, and slowly pull the newspaper and book toward you. Observe.

Easter Island *(Continued)*

5. Remove the newspaper. Place five pencils on the flat surface, arranged so they will all roll in the same direction. Place the textbook on the pencils.

6. Place your hand on the textbook and slowly push the book across the surface in one direction. Observe.

Describe Your Results

1. What happened when you pushed the textbook on the table?

   _____

   _____

2. What happened when you pulled the newspaper and book toward you?

   _____

   _____

3. What happened when you pushed the textbook over the pencils?

   _____

   _____

What's the Solution?

Now that you have completed the lab, use what you learned to solve "The Mystery of Easter Island." Additional hint: Something that rolls or slides is considered a simple machine.

Exercises

Fill in the blanks with the correct answer:

1. _____ discovered Easter Island.
2. Easter Island was formed by three _____.
3. The Easter Island _____ are strange rock statues.

Easter Island *(Continued)*

True or False?

1. Easter Island is round in shape. _____

2. There are more than 600 statues on Easter Island.
   _____

3. This island is located 500 miles west of the United States.
   _____

4. Some of these statues weigh as much as several tons.
   _____

5. The civilization that carved these stone statues disappeared.
   _____

Unscramble these words from the activity:

1. CVLOCIAN _____
2. STEERA _____
3. KROW _____
4. ENOTS _____
5. EHDA _____

Extension

Another simple machine is called a lever. Look up the word *lever.* How might a lever have been used to move the stone heads of Easter Island?

34. The Mystery of the Deadly Lake

Lake Nyos is located in Cameroon in western central Africa. The lake sits in the crater of an old volcano and is very deep. One sad morning in 1984 every human and animal for many miles around the lake died. This terrible tragedy has been repeated many times over the years. What is it about this seemingly peaceful, ancient lake that periodically kills the people and animals living around its shores?

Lab: Heavy Gas

In this lab, we will examine the effects of a gas produced from simple kitchen products.

Materials

Glass
Small lump of modeling clay
Small birthday candle
Baking soda
Matches (for adult use only)
Vinegar

What to Do

1. Place the glass on a flat surface. Place the small lump of clay inside the bottom of the glass.
2. Set the candle upright inside the bottom of the glass.
3. Place 3 tablespoons of baking soda around the candle.
4. Have an adult light the candle.
5. Pour enough vinegar around the base of the candle to completely cover the baking soda. Observe.

Deadly Lake *(Continued)*

Describe Your Results

1. What happened when the vinegar and baking soda were mixed?

   _____

   _____

2. What eventually happened to the lighted candle?

   _____

   _____

3. What eventually happened to the bubbles?

   _____

   _____

What's the Solution?

Now that you have completed the lab, use what you have discovered to solve "The Mystery of the Deadly Lake." Additional hints: Mixing vinegar and baking soda produces carbon dioxide gas. Also, look at the title of the lab for another hint.

Exercises

Fill in the blank with the correct answer:

1. Lake Nyos is in _____ in western central Africa.
2. The lake sits in the crater of an old _____.
3. In 1984, every _____ and human around the lake was killed.
4. Mixing vinegar and baking soda produces _____ _____.

Deadly Lake *(Continued)*

True or False?

1. Lake Nyos is in South America. _____

2. The tragedy at Lake Nyos has happened many times over the years.
   _____

3. The animals weren't affected by what happened in 1984.
   _____

4. The water of Lake Nyos is very shallow. _____

Unscramble these words from the activity:

1. OSNY _____
2. NOCRAB _____
3. YDAEDL _____
4. DIXODEI _____
5. RVENIGA _____

Extension

Repeat the experiment but this time without the candle. Using bubble solution, blow some bubbles so they land inside the glass as the baking soda and vinegar are reacting. What did you observe?

35. The Mystery of Magnetic Hill

In New Brunswick, Canada, in a normal country setting of rolling hills, there is one particular hill that seems to have strange magnetic properties. If you drive a car from the top of the hill to the bottom, put the car in neutral, and turn off the engine, the car will roll back up the hill on its own pulled by some mysterious force! How could this be possible?

Lab: Seeing Is Believing

In this lab, we'll examine how ordinary objects can be made to seem strange by slightly changing the area around them.

Materials

Scissors

Ruler

What to Do

1. Look at Diagram A (Arc 1 and Arc 2). Which looks bigger, Arc 1 or Arc 2?

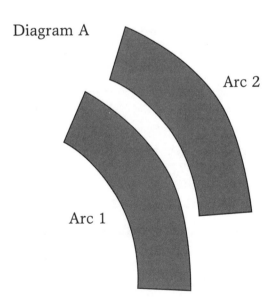

Diagram A

Arc 2

Arc 1

2. Copy and cut out Arc 1 and Arc 2 and compare their size by placing Arc 1 over Arc 2.

Magnetic Hill *(Continued)*

3. Look at the hat in Diagram B. Does the width of the hat's brim look like it's equal to the height of the hat?

4. Use a ruler to measure the width of the brim and the height of the hat.

Diagram B

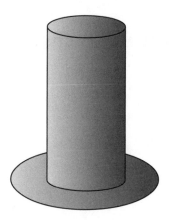

Describe Your Results

1. In Diagram A, which arc looks bigger?

_____

2. How do the arcs compare when they are laid on top of each other?

_____

_____

3. In Diagram B, does the width of the hat's brim look equal to the height of the hat?

_____

4. How do the actual measurements of the hat's width and height compare?

_____

_____

Magnetic Hill *(Continued)*

What's the Solution?

Now that you have completed the lab, use what you have learned to solve "The Mystery of Magnetic Hill."

Exercises

Fill in the blank with the correct answer:

1. Magnetic Hill is located in _____, Canada.
2. The hill seems to have strange _____ properties.
3. A car put in neutral at the bottom of the hill will _____ the hill unaided.

True or False?

1. Magnetic Hill is found in flat farm country. _____
2. Magnetic Hill seems to have strange properties.

   _____

3. Cars on Magnetic Hill cannot be put in neutral gear.

   _____

Unscramble these words from the activity:

1. CMIAGNTE _____
2. LIHL _____
3. MTOBTO _____
4. CRA _____
5. ROFEC _____

Extension

Look at this picture. What do you see? Change the position or angle at which you are looking at the picture. Now what do you see?

36. The Mystery of the C.S.S. Hunley

During the American Civil War, the Confederates were able to acquire a submarine—the C.S.S. *Hunley*. The submarine was powered by eight men, who turned a hand crank attached to a propeller. It could only stay submerged for 25 minutes before its oxygen ran out! The submarine was armed with a spar torpedo—a bundle of gunpowder at the end of a long pole jutting out from the nose of the boat. The *Hunley* completed its first mission on February 17, 1864, by blowing up and sinking the Union frigate *Housatonic* at the mouth of Charleston harbor. It was the first time a submarine ever succeeded in sinking an enemy ship in combat. The *Hunley* briefly surfaced, and the crew signaled that the mission was a success, but the ship never returned to port. All hands were presumed lost. In 1995, the *Hunley* was found and later raised. The crew had perished after completing their mission. What happened to this unique vessel and its crew?

Lab: Fire Breathing (Teacher Demonstration)

In this lab, we'll examine what happens to a candle without oxygen. A candle was used on the *Hunley* to be sure there was enough oxygen in the ship.

Materials

Small pan

Glass that fits over candle

Matches (for adult use only)

Candle

Small piece of modeling clay

What to Do

1. Place a small amount of modeling clay in the bottom of the pan.
2. Place the candle upright in the modeling clay. Pour enough water into the pan to cover the bottom of the candle.
3. Light the candle and invert the glass tumbler over the candle so it rests on the bottom of the pan. Observe what happens.

C.S.S. Hunley *(Continued)*

Describe Your Results

1. What happened to the candle flame when the glass tumbler was placed over the lighted candle?

   _____

   _____

2. What happened to the level of water?

   _____

   _____

What's the Solution?

Now that you have completed the lab, use what you have learned to solve "The Mystery of the C.S.S. *Hunley.*" Additional hint: In addition to fuel, what does fire need to burn?

Exercises

Fill in the blank with the correct answer:

1. The C.S.S. *Hunley* was a Confederate _____.
2. The craft was propelled by _____ turning a hand crank.
3. The *Hunley* was the first sub to _____ an enemy ship in combat.
4. The submarine was armed with a _____.
5. The C.S.S. *Hunley* never returned to _____.

C.S.S. *Hunley* (Continued)

True or False?

1. The C.S.S. *Hunley* was a Union submarine. _____

2. The *Hunley* could remain submerged for several hours.

   _____

3. The Union frigate *Housatonic* was sunk by the *Hunley*.

   _____

4. The sunken *Hunley* was discovered in 1995 and later raised.

   _____

Unscramble these words from the activity:

1. YLHENU _____

2. CELDAN _____

3. ESBURAMNI _____

4. LIVCI RWA _____

5. ETREDECNOFA _____

Extensions

1. A famous author found the *Hunley*. Discover who this author was.

2. Fire cannot survive without three things. This is called the fire triangle. What are the three parts of the fire triangle?

37. The Mystery of the Dancing Stones of Death Valley

Death Valley is a desert section of California where the temperature often soars to over 125 degrees during the summer months. During the winter, however, it gets very cold at night, sometimes even below freezing, and it occasionally rains on the sandy ground. There are also strong winds through the valley, which drops to a depth of approximately 1 mile below sea level.

A part of the valley known as Racetrack Playa contains countless boulders ranging in size from a few pounds to many hundreds of pounds. These boulders seem to move mysteriously by themselves, but no one has ever seen these rocks actually move! The tracks of these "dancing stones" vary in length from a few inches to many, many feet. How can these stones in this extreme environment seemingly move and make tracks without any outside help?

Lab: Slip Sliding Away

In this lab, we'll examine the effects of several liquids on friction.

Materials

Three sheets of tagboard

Three textbooks

Baby oil

Corn oil

Motor oil

Four identical wooden blocks

Stopwatch or digital watch

Eyedropper

Dancing Stones of Death Valley *(Continued)*

What to Do

1. Make a ramp with the tagboard by putting one end on a pile of textbooks.
2. Place a wooden block on the ramp and use a stopwatch to time its descent down to the bottom of the ramp.
3. Place three drops of corn oil on the bottom of one of the wooden blocks.
4. Place the block on top of the ramp and use the stopwatch to time its descent to the bottom of the ramp.
5. Repeat, using the third wooden block with three drops of baby oil on the bottom.
6. Repeat, using the fourth wooden block with three drops of motor oil on the bottom.

Describe Your Results

1. How many seconds did it take the clean wooden block to slide down the tagboard ramp? _____
2. How many seconds did it take the wooden block with corn oil on the bottom to slide down the tagboard ramp? _____
3. How many seconds did it take the block with the baby oil on the bottom to slide down the tagboard ramp? _____
4. How many seconds did it take the block with the motor oil on the bottom to slide down the tagboard ramp? _____

What's the Solution?

Now that you have completed your lab, use what you discovered to solve "The Mystery of the Dancing Stones of Death Valley."

Exercises

Fill in the blank with the correct answer:

1. Death Valley is _____ below sea level.
2. The temperature in the summer often soars to over _____ degrees Fahrenheit.
3. During the winter months the temperature at Racetrack Playa can drop below _____.
4. No one has ever seen the rocks actually _____.

Dancing Stones of Death Valley *(Continued)*

True or False?

1. Death Valley is located in California. _____

2. The stones at Racetrack Playa weigh only a few ounces. _____

3. The surface at Racetrack Playa is composed of sand particles. _____

4. It never rains in Death Valley. _____

Unscramble these words from the activity:

1. ATEH _____
2. NFOIRTCI _____
3. YELLAV _____
4. HDETA _____
5. OTSENS _____

Extension

Why is it important to an engine that motor oil reduces friction?

38. The Mystery of Drowning in Quicksand

We have probably all seen a movie scene in which a person running through a swampy area suddenly becomes trapped in quicksand. The victim slowly sinks into the muck until the last we see of this unfortunate person is an outstretched hand as it disappears out of sight.

Quicksand is real. It's a mixture of sand and water. But could a person really drown in quicksand?

Lab: To Float or Not to Float?

In this lab, we'll examine density and buoyancy. Density (a measure of mass per unit of volume) is how closely or loosely packed the molecules of a substance are. Buoyancy is a force. When something is placed in water, the water pushes back on that object. The degree to which the object floats is known as its buoyancy.

Materials

Bucket

Can of regular soda

Can of diet soda of the same brand

Several other assorted cans of soda

Clear plastic cup

Water

Hardboiled egg with shell

Salt

Stirrer or spoon

What to Do

Activity 1

1. Fill the bucket with water and place a can of regular soda into the bucket. Draw a diagram of the soda and its floating position in the water.

2. Do the same for the diet soda.

3. Do the same for each of the other sodas.

Drowning in Quicksand *(Continued)*

Activity 2

1. Fill a clear plastic cup about two-thirds full with water.
2. Carefully place a hardboiled egg into the water. Observe.
3. Remove the egg and stir salt into the water until no more salt dissolves.
4. Place the hardboiled egg into the water. Observe.

Describe Your Results

1. In Activity 1, how does the floating position of the diet soda compare with that of the regular soda of the same brand?

   _____

   _____

2. Which soda type floats highest?

   _____

   _____

3. Which soda type floats lowest?

   _____

   _____

4. Water has a density of 1.0. Are the densities of each of the sodas more or less than 1.0?

   _____

   _____

5. In Activity 2, what happened when you first placed the egg into the water in the cup?

   _____

   _____

Drowning in Quicksand *(Continued)*

6. What happened when you placed the egg into the salty water?

_____

_____

What's the Solution?

Now that you have completed the lab, use what you have learned to solve "The Mystery of Drowning in Quicksand." Additional hint: Quicksand is denser than water.

Exercises

Fill in the blank with the correct answer:

1. In movies, you sometimes see people _____ in quicksand.
2. Quicksand is sand that is mixed with _____.
3. The ability to float is called _____.

True or False?

1. Quicksand isn't real. _____
2. Density can be explained as how close or loosely the molecules of a substance are packed together. _____
3. Buoyancy is a force. _____

Unscramble these words from the activity:

1. OABYYCUN _____
2. CEFRO _____
3. YDSINET _____
4. TOLAF _____
5. SNADCKQIU _____

Extension

Place an egg in diet soda and regular soda. What happened?

39. The Mystery of the *Hindenburg*

The *Hindenburg* was the largest airship ever built, a type of ship known as a zeppelin, which was like a modern blimp. But unlike a blimp, which is filled with helium, a nonexplosive gas, the huge gas cells of the *Hindenburg* were filled with hydrogen, a very explosive gas. Below the teardrop shape of the airship was a gondola that carried passengers and crew in luxurious comfort.

On May 6, 1937, trying to bypass many lightning storms in the area, the *Hindenburg* exploded as it was landing at Lakehurst, New Jersey. The explosion of the *Hindenburg* was one of the first times a disaster was recorded on radio and film. Because it was such a newsworthy event, news and radio reporters plus film crews were present at the landing as it plummeted to the ground in flames. There were many safety devices inside the airship to guard against this disaster, so how did it happen?

Lab: Flammable (Teacher Demonstration)

In this lab, we'll examine the flammability of various materials.

Materials

Candle with holder

Matches (for adult use only)

Metal tongs

Two aluminum pie plates

Small piece of aluminum foil

Small piece of wood

Small piece of cotton fabric

What to Do

1. Set the candle with holder on a table and light the candle.
2. Use the metal tongs to hold the small piece of aluminum foil in the flame for twenty seconds. Observe.
3. When finished place the hot material into the aluminum pie plate.
4. Repeat steps 2 and 3 with the small piece of wood.
5. Repeat steps 2 and 3 with the small piece of cotton fabric. (Use the second pie plate to extinguish the burning fabric.)

Hindenburg *(Continued)*

Describe Your Results

1. What happened to the small piece of aluminum foil when it was put in the candle flame?

   _____

   _____

2. What happened to the small piece of wood when it was put in the candle flame?

   _____

   _____

3. What happened to the small piece of cotton fabric when it was put in the candle flame?

   _____

   _____

What's the Solution?

Now that you have completed the lab, use what you have discovered to solve "The Mystery of the *Hindenburg*." Additional hints: The *Hindenburg* had a superstructure, a frame made of aluminum, to support its huge size. Many of the interior parts of the airship were made from wood. The whole outside surface of the airship was covered with a cotton linen fabric coated with a very flammable lacquer hardening material.

Exercises

Fill in the blank with the correct answer:

1. The *Hindenburg* was the largest _____ ever built.
2. The *Hindenburg* was a type of ship known as a _____.
3. The airship was filled with _____.
4. Modern blimps are filled with _____.
5. The *Hindenburg* crashed on _____, 1937.

Hindenburg *(Continued)*

True or False?

1. The gondola of the airship was very luxurious.

   _____

2. The airship exploded while landing at Philadelphia, Pennsylvania.

   _____

3. There were lightning storms in the area when the *Hindenburg* crashed. _____

4. The *Hindenburg* had a superstructure made of wood.

   _____

5. The disaster was recorded on radio and film.

   _____

Unscramble these words from the activity:

1. PNZILEPE _____
2. REDSSITA _____
3. NTTCOO _____
4. NOISPOEXL _____
5. NBRU _____

Extension

Before the *Hindenburg* disaster, another airship, which had an impressive safety record, made many transatlantic flights. What was the name of this airship and what were some of its many accomplishments?

40. The Mystery of the Giant Pictures

In South America an ancient people drew hundreds of gigantic pictures in the ground high up on a desert plain between the Inca and Nazca valleys in Peru. Some of the lines of these pictures are several miles in length. These pictures, which are also called the Nazca lines, still exist and can best be seen from an airplane looking down from high up in the air.

On this plain in an area measuring 37 miles long and about 15 miles wide, there are straight lines, trapezoid shapes, strange symbols, and pictures of birds and animals. Scientists believe they were created between 200 and 150 B.C. Some people think that the drawings were made by extraterrestrials (aliens) who came to Earth long ago, but they were really produced by the Nazca people, an early Peruvian culture.

Today we can only guess how these drawings were made and what their purpose was. How might these ancient people have made the images without the help of modern machines?

Lab: Copy Cat

In this lab, we will examine an interesting technique for enlarging an image.

Materials

Cartoon from newspaper or comic book

Several sheets of graph paper of different grid size

Cellophane tape

Pencil

Ruler

What to Do

1. Cut a small cartoon out of a newspaper or comic.

2. Place the cartoon on a sheet of small-grid graph paper and tape it down.

3. Use the ruler and pencil to extend the graph paper's grid lines across the cartoon.

4. Label the vertical (up and down) boxes of the cartoon grid A, B, C, D, E, and so forth until you reach the end of the cartoon.

5. Label the horizontal (left and right) boxes of the cartoon grid 1, 2, 3, 4, and so forth until you reach the end of the cartoon.

Giant Pictures *(Continued)*

6. On a second sheet of graph paper with larger spaces, copy the same numbered and lettered grid without the cartoon.

7. Look at the A1 box on your cartoon. Copy exactly what you see onto the second grid with no cartoon.

8. Repeat this with A2, A3, and so on until you have completed that row.

9. Now go to the next row, B1, B2, B3, and so forth. Continue with the C row, the D row, and so on until you reach the end of the cartoon.

10. Look at the finished picture.

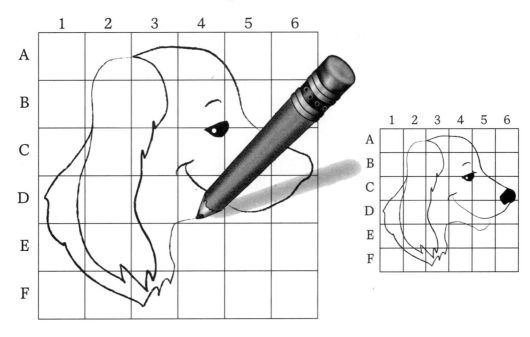

Describe Your Results

1. What happened when you copied your cartoon onto the larger grid?

_____

_____

2. Why is it important that you copy exactly what you see in each box?

_____

_____

Giant Pictures *(Continued)*

What's the Solution?

Now that you have completed the lab, use what you have discovered to solve "The Mystery of the Giant Pictures."

Exercises

Fill in the blank with the correct answer:

1. The Giant Pictures are located in the country of
   _____.

2. Some of the pictures are several _____ in length.

3. These drawings were made by the _____ people.

4. The drawings were made between about _____ and
   _____ B.C.

True or False?

1. Some of the Giant Pictures are of animals. _____

2. These pictures are found in Argentina. _____

3. The Giant Pictures date back to 150 to 200 years ago.
   _____

4. Some people think extraterrestrials constructed these pictures.
   _____

Unscramble these words from the activity:

1. REUCPIT _____
2. WDRA _____
3. SLEIN _____
4. TNGIA _____
5. CANZA _____

Extension

Use this technique to make a poster-size drawing of your cartoon.

41. The Mystery of Stonehenge

In southern England there is a group of huge, rough-cut, rectangular stones, which stand upright on end in the middle of a large plain. The stones are arranged in a circle, with some resting on top of two others and linking the circle together. Each stone is approximately 14 to 22 feet high and weighs up to 28 tons. Other stones arranged inside the circle are taller and heavier. Historians believe that Stonehenge was built over 4,000 years ago, possibly for astronomical observations. How were these ancient stones put in place with simple ancient tools?

Lab: Oof!

In this lab, you'll examine the effect of using a simple machine called an inclined plane, or a ramp, to help move an object.

Materials

Four identical textbooks

10-inch length of string

Four-legged table

Spring scale

Any small object, such as a toy car, rock, or piece of wood

Masking tape

What to Do

1. Place the small object on the table. Attach one end of the string to the small object with masking tape and tie one end to the spring scale.

2. Slowly lift the spring scale, with the object attached, about 6 inches off the table. Record the weight of the force needed to lift the object into the air with the spring scale.

3. Place two textbooks under each leg at one end of the table to raise the table evenly at one end.

Stonehenge *(Continued)*

4. Place the small object still attached to the spring scale at the lower end of the table. Slowly pull the object up the inclined plane by using the spring scale. Record the weight of the force used to pull the small object up the slope.

Describe Your Results

1. How much force (weight) did it take to pull the object straight up into the air?

_____

2. How much force (weight) did it take to pull the small object up the inclined plane?

_____

3. What was the difference between the two measurements?

_____

What's the Solution?

Now that you have completed the lab, use what you have discovered to solve "The Mystery of Stonehenge."

Exercises

Fill in the blank with the correct answer:

1. Stonehenge is in _____.
2. The stones weighed up to _____.
3. All the stones at Stonehenge are arranged in a
_____.

Stonehenge *(Continued)*

4. The simple machine examined in the lab is called an

_____

or _____ .

5. In the lab, a _____
is used to measure the force used on the inclined plane.

True or False?

1. Stonehenge is located in southern England. _____

2. Stonehenge was built 400 years ago. _____

3. Simple ancient tools were used to place the stones into place.
_____

4. An inclined plane is a ramp. _____

5. Stonehenge may have been used for astronomical observations or
worship. _____

Unscramble these words from the activity:

1. PRAM _____

2. EPALN _____

3. EGHESNOTEN _____

4. DGENLNA _____

5. NSOTSE _____

Extension

What do you think would happen if the ramp were made steeper? Try it.

42. The Mystery of the Dragons of China

The Chinese civilization dates back thousands of years. The ancient people of this land believed in dragons. There have been thousands of stories, legends, and pictures of these strange creatures. Chinese manuscripts describe using dragon blood and brains for medical remedies. Ground-up "dragon bones and teeth" have been used for teas and as a cure for ailments such as convulsions, paralysis, and ulcers. People claim to have found these "dragon bones" in deserts, such as the Gobi Desert in Mongolia. But dragons are mythical creatures, so how could the Chinese people obtain the bones of what they believed to be dragons?

Lab: You Old Fossil!

In this lab, we'll examine how a mold and cast can produce something called a "fossil." A fossil is the remains or impression of a creature that died a long time ago. Common fossils include seashells, dinosaur tracks in stone, dinosaur bones and teeth, dinosaur eggs, imprints of plants in stone, and fossilized dinosaur poop! In a fossil, the original material (bone, teeth, seashells, and dinosaur poop) becomes replaced by minerals, making them into stone.

Materials

Small amount of modeling clay

Small paper cup

An object that will fit into the cup, such as a key, a seashell, or coin

Plaster of paris or Permanentcast (can be purchased from science supply companies)

Water

What to Do

1. Place a small amount of modeling clay—about one inch deep—in the bottom of the paper cup.
2. Lightly smooth the top of the clay with your fingers.
3. Place the object firmly into the clay so it will make a deep, sharp, and clear impression. This is called a mold.

Dragons of China *(Continued)*

4. Remove the object carefully.

5. Mix the plaster of paris or use the premixed Permanentcast.

6. Pour the plaster material into the cup to a level two or three inches above the clay.

7. Allow the plaster to dry overnight.

8. The next day, carefully tear the paper material away from the plaster and clay. Remove the clay from the plaster. Observe. The hardened plaster is called a cast.

Describe Your Results

1. Describe what you observed when you removed the object from the clay.

   _____

   _____

2. Describe what you observed when you removed the paper and clay from the hardened plaster.

   _____

   _____

3. What percentage (50 percent or 100 percent) of your "fossil" was reproduced in the cast?

   _____

   _____

4. Could you identify your object if this was all you had to examine?

   _____

   _____

What's the Solution?

Now that you have completed your lab, use what you have discovered to solve "The Mystery of the Dragons of China." Additional hint: Many dinosaur fossils have been found in China.

Dragons of China *(Continued)*

Exercises

Fill in the blank with the correct answer:

1. The ancient Chinese people believed in _____.

2. In China there have been thousands of _____, legends, and pictures of dragons.

3. The remains or imprint of a very old creature is called a _____.

4. The imprint produced in the clay is called a _____.

5. When the paper and clay are peeled away, what is left is called a _____.

True or False?

1. Molds and casts in nature can show evidence of past life. _____

2. Dinosaur poop is considered a fossil. _____

3. Some Chinese people ground up "dragon bones" for tea. _____

4. Fossil bones and teeth are actually stone. _____

Unscramble these words from the activity:

1. TSCA _____
2. HTETE _____
3. NGDROA _____
4. SNBOE _____
5. SFISOL _____

Extensions

1. Paint your cast.
2. Try making more fossil casts with other objects or a real fossil!

43. The Mystery of the Woman Who Didn't Drown

On July 24, 1915, the steamship *Eastland* was in a dock on the Chicago River getting ready for a trip to Michigan City, Indiana. She was carrying 2,500 Western Electric Company employees and their families to a company picnic. All on board were having a wonderful time watching a parade of smaller boats and other excursion vessels on the river. The passengers mainly gathered on one side of the vessel, and the *Eastland*, which had a history of instability and wasn't meant to carry such a crowd, began to roll and then capsized, throwing hundreds of passengers into the river. Rescue boats arrived at the scene and frantic men chopped holes into the capsized hull to extract the passengers who had been trapped inside the ship when it turned over. Approximately 800 people lost their lives in this disaster.

One woman's body was taken from a hole in the hull, covered with a blanket, and carried on a stretcher to shore. A rescuer noticed her arm move out from under the shroud. Upon investigation he found her to be alive! How was it possible for this woman to have survived when the part of the *Eastland* that she was taken from had been underwater for a long time?

Lab: Underwater Air

In this lab, we will investigate how air can be transferred underwater.

Materials

Plastic bucket

Water

Two small drinking glasses

What to Do

1. Fill the bucket with water.
2. Submerge one of the drinking glasses (glass 1). Allow the glass to fill completely with water and then turn it upside down inside the bucket so that it is still completely filled with water. Continue to hold glass 1 underwater with one hand.

Copyright © 2006 by John Wiley & Sons, Inc.

Woman Who Didn't Drown *(Continued)*

3. Turn the second drinking glass (glass 2) upside down and submerge it in the water.

4. Carefully tip glass 2 so that it's under glass 1. Observe what happens.

Describe Your Results

1. What happened when glass 1 was filled with water and was submerged into the bucket of water?

   _____

   _____

2. What happened when glass 2 was submerged in the bucket of water?

   _____

   _____

3. What happened when you tipped glass 2 while it was under glass 1?

   _____

   _____

What's the Solution?

Now that you have completed the lab, use what you discovered to solve "The Mystery of the Woman Who Didn't Drown."

Exercises

Fill in the blank with the correct answer:

1. The name of the excursion steamship was the _____.

2. The *Eastland* was docked in the _____ River.

3. Approximately _____ people lost their lives in the disaster.

4. The rescuer knew the woman was alive because he saw her _____ move.

Woman Who Didn't Drown *(Continued)*

True or False?

1. The *Eastland* disaster occurred in May of 1955. _____

2. The steamship capsized on its way to the Western Electric Company picnic. _____

3. The steamship was carrying 250 people. _____

4. The rescuers chopped holes in the hull of the ship to extract people. _____

Unscramble these words from the activity:

1. SPHTEMAIS _____
2. PPTDERA _____
3. LDNATSEA _____
4. NOAMW _____
5. RWEAT _____

Extension

Learn more about the survivors of the *Eastland* disaster. What was the most famous disaster that occurred on water? (Hint: See Activity 63.) How many people survived that disaster?

44. The Mystery of the Sargasso Sea

The Sargasso Sea is a mysterious, deep blue, oval-shaped sea, hundreds of square miles in area, which is part of the North Atlantic Ocean. This unusual sea is dotted with many clumps of seaweed. In spring and summer, there are so many patches of floating seaweed that the clumps form huge fields of seaweed. Because the sea is so calm, sailors used to think their ships were being trapped by the seaweed.

The Sargasso Sea rotates clockwise, very slowly, and marks the meeting and melding of major warm Atlantic currents and winds. The Sargasso Sea is much warmer and calmer than the ocean waters that surround it, and it is pushed up about three feet higher than the surrounding ocean.

Why is the Sargasso Sea blanketed with seaweed, and why is it higher, calmer, and warmer than the surrounding ocean?

Lab: Push Up

In this lab, we'll examine how water behaves under different conditions.

Materials

Mixing bowl	Pennies
Eggbeater with crank	Water
Cellophane tape	Sink or deep dishpan
A glass	

What to Do

Activity 1

1. Pour water into the mixing bowl until the bowl is half full. Mark the level of the water in the bowl with a piece of cellophane tape.

2. Lower the blades of the eggbeater into the water and crank the beater.

3. Watch what happens to the water level because of the churning action of the eggbeater.

Sargasso Sea *(Continued)*

Activity 2

1. Fill the water glass with water just up to the rim of the glass. Do not allow any water to spill over the edges of the glass.

2. Slide pennies—one at a time—into the glass of water.

3. Watch the surface of the water curve up over the rim of the glass without spilling over.

Activity 3

1. Fill a sink or a deep dishpan halfway with cold water.

2. Slowly add warm water.

3. Use your fingers to feel the transfer of heat from the hot water to the cold water.

Describe Your Results

1. In Activity 1, what happened to the level of the water in the bowl when you cranked the beater?

   _____

   _____

2. In Activity 2, what happened each time you slid a coin into the water glass that was filled with water just up to its rim?

   _____

   _____

3. In Activity 3, what happened to the cold water in the sink, or dishpan, when you added warm water to the cold water?

   _____

   _____

Sargasso Sea *(Continued)*

What's the Solution?

Now that you have completed the lab, use what you discovered to solve "The Mystery of the Sargasso Sea."

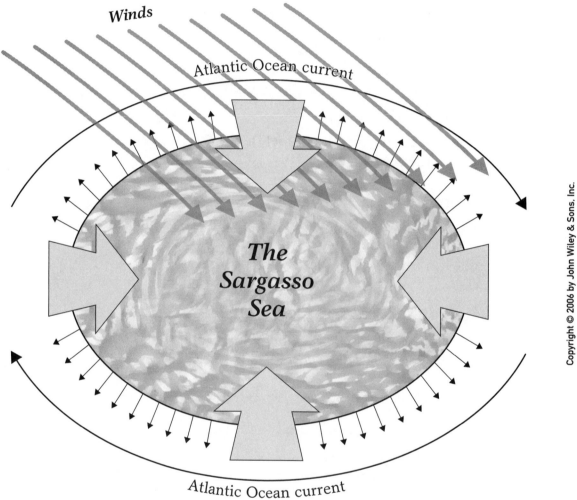

Winds

Atlantic Ocean current

The Sargasso Sea

Atlantic Ocean current

Exercises

Fill in the blank with the correct answer:

1. The Sargasso Sea is a mysterious sea that is dotted with clumps of
   _____ .

2. In spring and _____ , there are so many patches of floating seaweed that fields of seaweed are formed.

Sargasso Sea *(Continued)*

3. The Sargasso Sea marks the meeting and melding of major, warm Atlantic _____.

4. The Sargasso Sea is _____ and calmer than the ocean waters around it.

5. The Sargasso Sea is pushed up about _____ feet higher than the ocean that surrounds it.

True or False?

1. The Sargasso Sea is in the South Pacific Ocean. _____

2. The deep blue, oval-shaped waters of the Sargasso Sea are much warmer than the ocean water that surrounds it. _____

3. The Sargasso Sea is dotted with many clumps of seaweed.

   _____

4. The Sargasso Sea rotates very slowly clockwise. _____

5. In fall and winter, the Sargasso Sea has so many patches of floating seaweed that the clumps form huge fields of seaweed.

   _____

Unscramble these words from the activity:

1. SARSOGAS ASE _____
2. ORNTH TICLANAT _____
3. ASEDEWE _____
4. OCKCLSIWE _____
5. RUCRENTS _____

Extension

Research the major Atlantic currents that meet to form the Sargasso Sea.

45. The Mystery of the Ice Fences of the Himalayas

The world's highest mountains are the Himalayas in the countries of India, Nepal, and China as well as Tibet, which is now part of China. The highest of the Himalaya Mountains are well over 20,000 feet high, including the tallest mountain in the world, Mount Everest, which soars to 29,028 feet.

High winds and bitter cold make the Himalaya Mountains a challenging environment, especially in winter. It has been reported that there are fields of ice in the Himalaya Range that have borders of vertical pieces of ice up to ten feet high. These ice pickets are widest at their bases and taper gradually up to sharply pointed tops. They look something like huge stalagmites, and standing side-by-side they form mysterious ice fences.

What causes these enormous ice fences?

Lab: Goose Bumps

In this lab, we'll examine how snowdrifts form.

Materials

Sheet of newspaper

Table salt (about 26 ounces)

What to Do

1. Spread the sheet of newspaper on a table.

2. Pour a pile of salt onto the newspaper.

3. Hold your chin somewhat below the edge of the table, and blow a blast of your breath once—horizontally and sharply—across the tabletop toward the salt. Observe.

4. Continue to blow blasts of your breath to pile up the salt and create valleys between the piles. Observe.

5. Now blow another blast of your breath, and observe the way some salt slides down the sloping sides of the piles.

Ice Fences of the Himalayas *(Continued)*

Describe Your Results

1. What happened when you blew a blast of your breath once—sharply and horizontally—toward the salt?

   _____

   _____

2. What happened when you blew blasts of your breath to pile up the salt?

   _____

   _____

3. What happened when you blew a final blast of your breath to make salt slide?

   _____

   _____

4. Describe the shape of the piles of salt you made.

   _____

   _____

What's the Solution?

Now that you have completed the lab, use what you discovered to solve "The Mystery of the Ice Fences of the Himalayas."

Exercises

Fill in the blank with the correct answer:

1. The Himalayas are the world's _____ mountains.
2. There are mountains in the Himalayas that are well over _____ feet high.
3. Mount _____, at 29,028 feet, is the tallest mountain in the world.

Ice Fences of the Himalayas *(Continued)*

4. There are _____ of ice in the Himalayas that have borders of ice pickets.

5. The ice pickets are up to _____ feet high.

True or False?

1. The world's highest mountains are America's Rocky Mountains.
   _____

2. The tallest of the Himalaya Mountains are well over 20,000 feet high. _____

3. There is very little wind in the Himalayas. _____

4. There are fields of ice in the Himalaya Range that have borders of ice pickets that are up to ten feet tall. _____

5. Ice pickets have narrow bases that widen gradually up to their tops.
   _____

Unscramble these words from the activity:

1. TAINMOUNS _____
2. LAMAIHSYA _____
3. CIE KICTPSE _____
4. MOTNU ESEVETR _____
5. SCENEF _____

Extension

Find out more about conditions in the Himalayas. Why do climbers on Mount Everest need to carry oxygen tanks?

46. The Mystery of the Flash Point

Firefighters make every effort, whenever it is possible, to fight a fire from inside a burning building. Spraying water onto a burning building from outside the building is not always effective. But it's very dangerous to be inside a building that is on fire because you never know when the fire might suddenly accelerate. It is terrifying when a room in a blazing building experiences the flash point, the point when almost everything in the room suddenly explodes into flames at the same time.

What causes the flash point?

Lab: Flash! (Teacher Demonstration)

In this lab, we'll examine how fuel ignites a fire.

Materials

Sheet of aluminum foil

Wax candle, preferably a fairly thick candle (do not use a birthday cake candle)

Wooden kitchen matches

What to Do

1. Light the candle over the sheet of aluminum foil (to catch any drips). Study the flame.

2. Allow the candle to burn for one or two full minutes, observing the wax surface at the top of the candle.

3. Blow out the candle flame.

4. Watch the curl of white smoke that rises from the wick of the candle.

5. Quickly push a burning match into the column of smoke at least six inches above the wick before the smoke disappears. Observe!

Flash Point *(Continued)*

Describe Your Results

1. Describe the flame of the burning candle.

   _____

   _____

2. What happened to the wax when you lit the candle?

   _____

   _____

3. What happened when you pushed a burning match into the curl of smoke that rose from the candle?

   _____

   _____

What's the Solution?

Now that you have completed the lab, use what you have discovered to solve "The Mystery of the Flash Point." Additional hint: The kindling temperature must be reached for fire to occur.

Exercises

Fill in the blank with the correct answer:

1. If it is possible, firefighters make every effort to fight a fire from _____ a burning building.

2. Spraying water onto a burning building from _____ the building is not always effective.

3. When a _____ in a burning building experiences the flash point, it is terrifying.

4. The _____ is the point when just about everything in a room in a blazing building explodes into flames at the same time.

Flash Point *(Continued)*

True or False?

1. Firefighters make every effort to fight a fire from inside a burning building if possible. _____

2. Spraying water onto a blazing building from outside the building is always effective. _____

3. It is terrifying when a room in a burning building experiences the flash point. _____

4. Just about everything in a room that experiences the flash point explodes into flames at the same time. _____

Unscramble these words from the activity:

1. AHFLS PTONI _____
2. EFRI _____
3. ERTAW _____
4. FEIGHTRIFER _____
5. OMOR _____

Extension

What can be done to try to contain the spread of the terrifying fire in a room that experiences the flash point?

47. The Mystery of the Island That Vanished

In 1831, a small island appeared in the Mediterranean Sea, southwest of Sicily. This island was named Graham Island, in honor of Sir James Graham, the First Lord of the British Admiralty. Graham Island came up from the sea, gushing smoke and fire, and gradually attained a height of more than one hundred feet above sea level and a diameter of about one-half mile.

By the end of the year, the island had disappeared. Can you figure out where it went?

Lab: Gone!

In this lab, we'll examine the qualities of volcanic rock, rock that is formed when lava from a volcano cools and hardens.

Scoria (rough, cindery lava) is a volcanic rock that has large vesicles or holes. These holes were filled with steam or other gasses when the volcano they came from erupted. Pumice is a volcanic rock that also has holes made by bubbles. Pumice is very light and can float in water. Scoria and pumice are both soft and easily crushed.

Materials

Slice of white bread

Magnifying glass

Newspaper

Brown sugar

Specimens of volcanic rock, such as scoria and pumice (available from a science supply company)

What to Do

Activity 1

1. Carefully examine the slice of bread with the magnifying glass.
2. Study the specimens of volcanic rock with the magnifying glass.

Island That Vanished *(Continued)*

Activity 2

1. Cover the top of a table with sheets of newspaper.
2. Pour brown sugar into a pile on the newspaper.
3. Shape the sugar into a cone-shaped pile.
4. Pound the tabletop lightly with your fists around the pile of brown sugar. What happened to the pile?

Describe Your Results

1. What did you see in the slice of bread with the magnifying glass?

   _____

   _____

2. What did you see in the volcanic rock samples with the magnifying glass?

   _____

   _____

3. What happened to the cone-shaped pile of brown sugar when you pounded your fists on the table?

   _____

   _____

What's the Solution?

Now that you have completed the lab, use what you discovered to solve "The Mystery of the Island That Vanished."

Exercises

Fill in the blank with the correct answer:

1. In _____, Graham Island appeared in the Mediterranean Sea.
2. Graham Island came up from the sea and gradually attained a height of more than one hundred feet above _____ .

Island That Vanished *(Continued)*

3. When the island rose from the sea, it gushed smoke and
   _____.

4. Graham Island had a _____ of about one-half mile.

5. By the end of the year, Graham Island had

   _____.

True or False?

1. In 1831, a small island, Graham Island, appeared in the Baltic Sea.
   _____

2. Graham Island was named in honor of Sir James Graham, the First
   Lord of the British Admiralty. _____

3. Graham Island came up from the sea, gushing fire and smoke.
   _____

4. The island gradually reached a height of more than five hundred
   feet. _____

5. By the end of 1831, Graham Island had disappeared.
   _____

Unscramble these words from the activity:

1. DITEMREARNEAN ESA _____
2. GAMRAH ILDSAN _____
3. SIDPAPARE _____
4. KOMES _____
5. ERIF _____

Extension

What causes a soufflé that is being baked in an oven to drop, or collapse,
when someone opens the oven door to take a peek?

48. The Mystery of the Circus Queen's Fall

Lillian Leitzel was a famous circus queen in the early twentieth century. An aerialist of matchless artistry, she performed her dangerous act without a safety net. Much of her performance was done on Roman rings, high in the air. A Roman ring is attached to a metal swivel at the bottom of a vertical rope hung from above.

At the end of her act, Lillian Leitzel hung high in the air by one arm from a padded loop with a metal swivel. She swung herself around, throwing her body over her right shoulder—in a circle—like a propeller. Early in her career, she could do this 150 times during each performance.

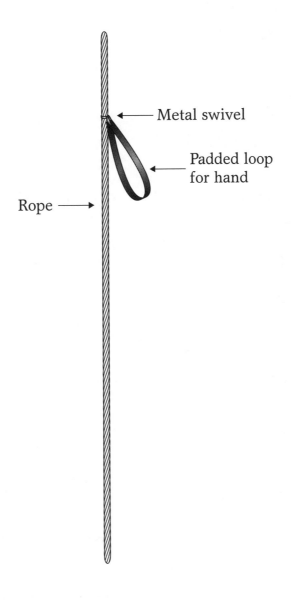

Metal swivel

Padded loop for hand

Rope

Circus Queen's Fall *(Continued)*

Then in 1931, at the end of a performance in Denmark, the metal swivel of her padded loop broke and Lillian fell twenty feet to the floor. Two days later, she died from complications.

Why might the solid metal swivel have suddenly broken, sending Lillian to her death?

Lab: Tired Metal

In this lab, we'll examine how the heat of friction from the repeated heating and cooling of a metal part can cause the part to break.

Materials

Plastic coated, metal twist tie

What to Do

Activity 1
1. Put your hands together and rub them hard and briskly. Observe.
2. Stop rubbing your hands and separate them. Observe.

Activity 2
1. Pick up the twist tie. Straighten the tie with your fingers, and then fold it in half.
2. Grip the twist tie firmly, and bend the tie back and forth where the wire is folded until it breaks and separates.

Describe Your Results

1. In Activity 1, what happened when you rubbed your hands together hard and briskly?

   _____

   _____

2. What happened when you stopped rubbing your hands together?

   _____

   _____

3. In Activity 2, what happened when you bent the twist tie back and forth?

   _____

_____

Circus Queen's Fall *(Continued)*

What's the Solution?

Now that you have completed your lab, use what you discovered to solve "The Mystery of the Circus Queen's Fall." Additional hints: Metal that is heated expands. Metal that is cooled contracts.

Exercises

Fill in the blank with the correct answer:

1. Lillian Leitzel was an _____ of matchless ability.
2. She performed without a _____ net.
3. Much of her performance was presented high in the air on _____.
4. A Roman ring is attached to a _____ at the bottom of a vertical rope hung from above.
5. At the end of her performance, Lillian Leitzel hung by one _____ high in the air from a padded loop with a metal swivel, and swung herself around.

True or False?

1. Lillian Leitzel was a well-known circus queen. _____
2. Lillian always performed with a safety net. _____
3. Much of her performance was done high in the air on a trapeze. _____
4. At the end of her act, Lillian hung high above the floor by one arm from a padded loop with a metal swivel. _____
5. In her last performance, Lillian Leitzel fell when the metal swivel of her padded loop broke. _____

Unscramble these words from the activity:

1. LANILLI LEZTEIL _____
2. ROMNA GRINS _____
3. FORMREPANCE _____
4. TALEM VELSWI _____
5. RUCSIC NEQUE _____

Extension

How can metal be made tougher to resist metal fatigue so that metal parts can be used safely for longer periods?

49. The Mystery of the Bouncing Cannonballs

The frigate U.S.S. *Constitution* is the oldest commissioned warship in the world that is still afloat. Launched in Boston, Massachusetts, in 1797, the *Constitution* had speed, excellent handling, and forty-four heavy cannons. Her hull could withstand the impact of enemy cannonballs, which just bounced away. This gave her the nickname "Old Ironsides," and she was believed to be a lucky ship.

Old Ironsides saw action against pirates in the Barbary wars of North Africa and against the British in the War of 1812. She was a gallant ship that, among many engagements, was never defeated. You can visit the U.S.S. *Constitution* where it is stationed at the Navy Yard in Charlestown, Massachusetts.

See whether you can discover why the *Constitution* was able to deflect enemy cannonballs.

Lab: Boom! Bang! (Teacher Demonstration)

In this lab, we'll examine how different types of wood are affected by a hammer blow.

Materials

Thick telephone directory

Three short lengths of different kinds of wood: maple, pine, and balsa (balsa wood may be available in a hobby shop; pine and maple pieces can be found in a store that sells lumber and other building supplies)

Hammer

What to Do

1. Put the telephone directory on a table. The thick telephone book absorbs the impact of the hammer that the teacher uses in this activity, and protects the tabletop as well.

2. Lay the piece of maple on the telephone book.

Bouncing Cannonballs *(Continued)*

3. Pick up the hammer and position its head about one foot over the piece of maple.
4. Strike the piece of maple with the hammer. Observe what happens to the wood.
5. Replace the piece of maple with the piece of pine.
6. Repeat the procedure. Carefully observe what happens to the pine.
7. Repeat the procedure with the piece of balsa wood.

Describe Your Results

1. What happened when the hammer struck the piece of maple?

   _____

   _____

2. What happened when the hammer struck the piece of pine?

   _____

   _____

3. What happened when the hammer struck the piece of balsa?

   _____

   _____

What's the Solution?

Now that you have completed the lab, use what you discovered to solve "The Mystery of the Bouncing Cannonballs."

Exercises

Fill in the blank with the correct answer:

1. The U.S.S. *Constitution* is nicknamed _____.
2. It is the oldest _____ warship still afloat in the world.
3. She was launched in 1797 in _____, Massachusetts.
4. The *Constitution* had speed, excellent _____, and forty-four heavy cannons.
5. The warship saw much action in the War of _____.

Bouncing Cannonballs *(Continued)*

True or False?

1. The U.S.S. *Constitution* is retired, and is no longer a commissioned warship. _____

2. The U.S.S. *Constitution* was launched in 1797 in Baltimore, Maryland. _____

3. Old Ironsides' nickname came from her iron hull. _____

4. Old Ironsides saw action against pirates in the Barbary wars of North Africa. _____

5. The U.S.S. *Constitution* was never defeated. _____

Unscramble these words from the activity:

1. DOL SIDRONIES _____
2. WRPHASI _____
3. CONANBANLLS _____
4. LUHL _____
5. OUBCNED _____

Extension

Why is it much safer for people to play in a gymnasium that has a wood floor instead of vinyl tiles on a concrete base?

50. The Mystery of the Mary Celeste

On December 4, 1872, the *Dei Gratia,* a sailing ship, sighted another ship, the *Mary Celeste,* in the distance at sea. The *Mary Celeste* was a small but sturdy ship that was not carrying much sail, and for some reason was sailing poorly.

The *Dei Gratia* sailed near the *Mary Celeste* and hailed her repeatedly but got no response. A boat was launched, and the *Mary Celeste* was boarded.

There was no one on the ship. The crew of seven plus the captain and his wife and their two-year-old daughter were all missing, along with the ship's only lifeboat and its navigation instruments.

One of the ship's pumps was damaged, and there was water in the hold. Nevertheless, the *Mary Celeste* was seaworthy. A cargo of 1,700 barrels of alcohol was stored in the hold. Eight of the barrels were empty. Two of the ship's three hatches were open.

There was no evidence that there had been any fire on the ship. Despite conflicting accounts, no blood was found on the *Mary Celeste,* and there were no signs of a struggle. A long, narrow strip of wood, however, was missing—mysteriously—from the ship's bow. A six-month's supply of food was on board, and the ship had plenty of drinking water.

The last entry in the ship's log was for November 24. The ship had sailed, apparently without a crew, between 500 and 750 miles in ten days—a most unusual voyage, which some say wouldn't have been made without someone manning the sails. The ten people who were missing, and their lifeboat, were never seen again.

What could have happened to the people who sailed on the *Mary Celeste?*

Lab: Without a Trace (Teacher Demonstration)

In this lab, we'll examine what happens to rubbing alcohol that is left out in a measuring cup overnight.

Mary Celeste *(Continued)*

Materials

Rubbing alcohol

Measuring cup

Pen or pencil

Sheet of paper

What to Do

1. Pour exactly two ounces of rubbing alcohol into a measuring cup.

2. Record the volume of the alcohol that you poured into the cup.

3. Leave the measuring cup with the alcohol in it out on a table overnight.

4. On the following day, use the ounce scale on the side of the cup to measure the volume of the alcohol.

5. Record your measurement.

6. Compare the two measurements that you recorded.

Describe Your Results

1. What had happened to the volume of the rubbing alcohol in the measuring cup by the second day of this activity?

   _____

   _____

2. What was the difference between the volume of alcohol in the cup on the first day and the volume of alcohol on the second day?

   _____

   _____

3. Where did the alcohol go?

   _____

   _____

What's the Solution?

Now that you have completed the lab, use what you discovered to solve "The Mystery of the *Mary Celeste.*"

Mary Celeste *(Continued)*

Exercises

Fill in the blanks with the correct answer:

1. The _____ was the ship that sighted the *Mary Celeste* and hailed her repeatedly.
2. The *Mary Celeste* was carrying a cargo of _____ in its hold.
3. The ship's lifeboat and _____ instruments were missing.
4. Two of the *Mary Celeste*'s _____ were open.
5. A narrow strip of _____ was missing from the bow of the ship's hull.

True or False?

1. The *Mary Celeste* carried a cargo of alcohol in its hold.
   _____

2. The *Dei Gratia* sighted the *Mary Celeste* in the distance at sea.
   _____

3. The *Mary Celeste* was a pirate ship. _____
4. The ten people who were on the *Mary Celeste* were missing and were never seen again. _____
5. The *Mary Celeste*'s lifeboat was found—in perfect condition—on a sandy shore. _____

Unscramble these words from the activity:

1. MYRA CELSTEE _____
2. ACOLOLH _____
3. THACH _____
4. IDE GARTAI _____
5. YOVGEA _____

Extension

Unlike the *Mary Celeste,* which carried its cargo of alcohol in barrels, how do today's modern ships transport cargoes of volatile, combustible liquids?

51. The Mystery of the Great Molasses Flood

On January 15, 1919, which was an unusually warm day for winter in Boston, Massachusetts, a big, outdoor, cast-iron storage tank containing 2.3 million gallons of molasses exploded.

A wall of molasses at least 8 feet (some said 15 feet) high rushed into Commercial Street, moving at a speed of 35 miles per hour. Warehouses were destroyed, freight cars were broken, and homes were left in ruins. Horses, which were still widely used to haul wagons at that time, were buried by molasses. Twenty-one people died, and more than 150 were injured. This tragic event was named the Great Molasses Flood. What might have caused this mysterious flood?

Lab: The Heat Is On

In this lab, we'll examine how heat affects objects.

Materials

Thermometer

Sheet of paper

Pencil or pen

Clean, empty glass bottle

Water

Coin

What to Do

Activity 1

1. Read the thermometer and record your reading on the sheet of paper.

2. Place the thermometer on a sunny windowsill.

3. After 15 minutes, read the thermometer again and record your reading on the sheet of paper.

4. Compare the readings.

Great Molasses Flood *(Continued)*

Activity 2

1. Store the bottle in a cool place for a while before the activity begins.
2. To begin the activity, moisten the rim of the mouth of the bottle with water.
3. Lay the coin on top of the bottle. Make sure that the coin covers the opening completely.
4. Grip the sides of the bottle with both hands. The palms of the hands should be placed flat against the sides of the bottle to facilitate the transfer of heat energy.
5. Wait patiently. Observe the coin. Watch and listen.

Describe Your Results

1. In Activity 1, what happened to the red liquid in the thermometer when you put the thermometer on a sunny windowsill?

   _____

   _____

2. In Activity 2, what happened to the coin on top of the bottle when you gripped the sides of the bottle with the palms of both hands?

   _____

   _____

What's the Solution?

Now that you have completed the lab, use what you discovered to solve "The Mystery of the Great Molasses Flood." Additional hint: When heated, molasses gives off alcohol vapors and heat.

Exercises

Fill in the blanks with the correct answer:

1. The Great Molasses Flood occurred on January 15,

   _____.

2. The weather that day was unusually _____ for winter in Boston.

Great Molasses Flood *(Continued)*

3. There were 2.3 million gallons of _____ stored in a big, outdoor tank.

4. The storage tank _____, and a wall of molasses rushed into Commercial Street.

5. Twenty-one people _____, and more than 150 were injured.

True or False?

1. On January 15, 1919, in Boston, Massachusetts, a big, outdoor, cast-iron storage tank exploded. _____

2. The tank contained 200 million gallons of molasses. _____

3. The rush of molasses buried horses, which were still widely used to haul wagons. _____

4. Fortunately, not one person lost his or her life in the flood. _____

5. This tragic event was named the Big, Brown Flood. _____

Unscramble these words from the activity:

1. OBSTNO _____
2. ERAGOST NKTA _____
3. OLASSEMS _____
4. PEXLOEDD _____
5. DOOFL _____

Extension

What could have been done to keep the cast-iron tank from exploding?

52. The Mystery of the Penny That Knows Whether You're a Girl or a Boy

A penny is attached to a light string and someone holds the string so the penny swings freely. A girl holds her extended hand, palm up, under the hanging penny. The coin begins to swing slowly in a circle over her hand. The penny is then held over a boy's upturned hand. This time the penny swings slowly back and forth in a straight line.

How does the suspended penny know whether it's hanging over a girl's hand or a boy's hand?

Lab: Hanging

In this lab, we'll examine what happens when we test a penny as described above.

Materials

Penny

6- or 7-inch length of light string (kite string works well)

Paste or glue

What to Do

1. Use paste or glue to attach one end of the string to the penny. Let the glue dry completely.
2. Hold the penny over a girl's extended hand, with her palm facing up.
3. Think "Girl." What happens to the penny?
4. Hang the penny over the palm of a boy's hand.
5. Think "Boy." What happens to the penny?

Penny That Knows Whether You're a Girl or a Boy *(Continued)*

Describe Your Results

1. What happened when you suspended the penny over a girl's extended hand with her palm facing up?

   _____

   _____

2. What happened when you suspended the penny over a boy's extended hand with his palm facing up?

   _____

   _____

What's the Solution?

Now that you have completed the lab, use what you discovered to solve "The Mystery of the Penny That Knows Whether You're a Girl or a Boy." Additional hint: Why does it matter what the person who is holding the string is thinking during the activity?

Exercises

Fill in the blanks with the correct answer:

1. When a penny is suspended over the palm of a girl's extended hand, the penny will swing slowly in a _____.
2. When a penny is suspended over the palm of a boy's extended hand, the penny will swing back and forth in a straight

   _____.
3. Both the boy's and girl's hands should be _____.
4. The penny seems to _____ whether it is hanging over the palm of a girl's or a boy's hand.

Penny That Knows Whether You're a Girl or a Boy *(Continued)*

True or False?

1. The suspended penny has the ability to think. _____

2. The coin swings in a circle over the palm of a girl's hand. _____

3. The coin swings in a straight line over the palm of a boy's hand. _____

Unscramble these words from the activity:

1. RINGST _____
2. PYENN _____
3. GRIL _____
4. OYB _____
5. MALP _____

Extension

What would happen to the penny if the person holding the string didn't think "Girl" or "Boy" or during the activity?

53. The Mystery of Nauscopie

M. Bottineau was an eighteenth-century lighthouse keeper on the Isle of France (now called Mauritius) in the Indian Ocean, who invented the art, or the science, of what he called nauscopie. *Naus* in Greek means "ship," and *scopie* is derived from the Greek word *skopos,* which means "a watcher."

According to M. Bottineau, nauscopie is based on a natural phenomenon. He believed that a cloud of colored vapors surrounds a moving ship, and that those vapors can be seen from far away—one, two, three, or four days before an approaching ship actually appears over the horizon. Using nauscopie, M. Bottineau claimed that he could determine whether one or more ships were sailing toward his island and the time that it would take for a ship to appear.

It was reported that from 1778 to 1782, M. Bottineau accurately announced the arrival of 575 ships before they became visible. These predictions were verified by other observers. The governor of the Isle of France and other officials of the then French-controlled island attested in writing to the accuracy of M. Bottineau's predictions. M. Bottineau insisted that nauscopie was the result of his careful observations of changes in the appearance of the air and the sky at the horizon. M. Bottineau wrote that the clear sky and the pure air of the Isle of France and its environs helped him in his observations.

Could nauscopie have a real scientific basis?

Lab: Colorful Spray

In this lab, we'll examine what happens when water is sprayed in the air on a sunny day and how air moves around objects.

Materials

Garden hose with a nozzle that can adjust the flow of water into a fine spray

Large, clean, empty bottle

Thick candle that will produce a good-sized flame

Candleholder

Matches (for adult use only)

What to Do

Activity 1

1. Go outside on a bright, sunny day. (This activity works early in the morning and late in the day when the sun's rays slant at the correct angle.)

Nauscopie *(Continued)*

2. Stand with the sun behind you.

3. Turn on the faucet connected to the hose and adjust the stream to a fine spray.

4. Direct the spray in the air and move it around until you see colors. Observe.

Activity 2

1. Stand the bottle upright on a table.

2. Stand the candle in the candleholder on the table about two inches behind the bottle.

3. Have an adult light the candle.

4. Blow air hard against the side of the bottle that is opposite the side where the candle is burning. Observe what happens.

Describe Your Results

1. In Activity 1, what did you see form in the fine spray of water?

   _____

   _____

2. In Activity 2, what happened when you blew hard at the bottle?

   _____

   _____

What's the Solution?

Now that you've completed the lab, use what you discovered to solve "The Mystery of Nauscopie." Additional hints: In the eighteenth century, the ships were sailing ships. A large sailing ship has many surfaces, such as sails, masts, and rigging, which create churning air, or turbulence, around them.

Exercises

Fill in the blanks with the correct answer:

1. M. Bottineau called his ability to announce the presence of ships before they appeared _____.

2. M. Bottineau invented nauscopie when he was stationed as a light-house keeper on the Isle of _____.

Nauscopie (Continued)

3. M. Bottineau claimed that he could determine whether one or more _____ were sailing toward his island before the ships actually appeared.

4. He also claimed that he could determine the _____ that it would take for an approaching ship to appear.

5. M. Bottineau insisted that nauscopie was the result of changes that he had carefully observed in the air and the sky at the

_____ .

True or False?

1. M. Bottineau was a lighthouse keeper. _____

2. M. Bottineau believed that a cloud of colored vapors surrounds a moving ship. _____

3. He always used a telescope to search the horizon for a ship that was approaching. _____

4. M. Bottineau said that the vapors surrounding a moving ship could be seen as much as four days before the approaching ship actually appears over the horizon. _____

5. M. Bottineau invented the telescope. _____

Unscramble these words from the activity:

1. COPINASUE _____
2. BINEATOTU _____
3. SIHSP _____
4. ZINHOOR _____
5. ORVAPS _____

Extension

How could nauscopie still be useful in today's world even though we now have radio, radar, sonar, and satellite technology?

54. The Mystery of Amelia Earhart's Disappearance

In 1932, Amelia Earhart became the first woman to pilot an airplane on her own across the Atlantic Ocean. As her next feat, she wanted to be the first pilot to fly around the world following the equator, which circles the widest part of the planet, so that she would be the first to fly the longest distance around the earth.

In 1937, in Miami, Florida, Amelia Earhart and Fred Noonan, a navigator, began their flight around the world, and one month later, with 22,000 miles of flying behind them, arrived in Lae, New Guinea. There were 2,556 miles from New Guinea to Howland, a speck of island in the vast Pacific Ocean that was to be the next stop on their journey. During the first 500 miles and the final 500 miles of this leg of the journey, Amelia Earhart and Fred Noonan could use their radio to determine their location. However, for 1,500 miles in between they would have to navigate by the stars at night, and by the sun in daylight. If it was cloudy, they might have to rely on their magnetic compass to navigate.

Amelia Earhart and Fred Noonan took off in New Guinea, headed toward Howland, and were never seen again. Amelia Earhart was last heard from when she radioed during the early morning hours of the day she was scheduled to land on Howland. She reported that the weather was cloudy and overcast.

What happened to Amelia Earhart and Fred Noonan?

Lab: Lost!

In this lab, we'll examine how a slight error in navigation can lead to a major deviation from the intended end point.

Materials

Pencil

Sheet of plain paper

Ruler

Protractor

Amelia Earhart's
Disappearance *(Continued)*

What to Do

1. Using the pencil and the ruler, draw a horizontal line about 2 inches long on the sheet of paper. Label the ends of the line A and B. Line AB is your base line.

2. Now draw a 2-inch perpendicular line from above that ends at a point in the middle of AB, the base line. Label the bottom end of the line C and the upper end of the line D.

3. Print beside point C the words "Lae, New Guinea." Print beside Point D the word "Howland."

4. Next, use the protractor to measure two degrees of arc immediately to the left of line CD and about one inch above AB, the base line. Mark this point and label it E.

5. Print beside point E the word "deviation."

6. Finally, draw a line from point C up to, and through, point E, and then extend this slanted line an additional 4 inches.

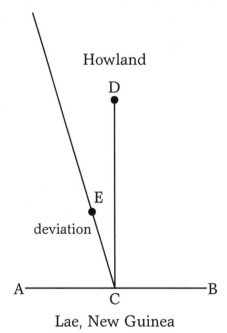

Describe Your Results

1. What does line CD represent?

_____

_____

Amelia Earhart's Disappearance *(Continued)*

2. What do line CE and its extension represent?

_____

_____

3. Why is point E labeled "deviation"?

_____

_____

4. What is the difference between lines CD and CE?

_____

_____

What's the Solution?

Now that you have completed the lab, use what you discovered to solve "The Mystery of Amelia Earhart's Disappearance."

Exercises

Fill in the blanks with the correct answer:

1. Amelia Earhart wanted to be the first pilot to fly the longest distance around the _____.

2. Amelia Earhart and Fred Noonan took one month to get from Miami, Florida to Lae, _____.

3. There are 2,556 miles between New Guinea and _____, a tiny island.

4. During the first 500 miles and the final 500 miles of this leg of the flight, Amelia Earhart and Fred Noonan would be able to use their _____.

5. For 1,500 miles, if the weather was clear, they would use the _____ to navigate at night and the sun in the daytime.

Amelia Earhart's Disappearance *(Continued)*

True or False?

1. Amelia Earhart was the first woman to pilot an airplane on her own across the Atlantic Ocean. _____

2. She wanted to be the first pilot to follow the equator, which circles the widest part of the earth, and to fly the longest distance around the world. _____

3. Amelia Earhart and Fred Noonan, her navigator, began their flight around the world in Chicago, Illinois. _____

4. One month later, with 22,000 miles behind them, they arrived in Lae, New Guinea. _____

5. Amelia Earhart and Fred Noonan, after many hours of flying, finally landed on Howland. _____

Unscramble these words from the activity:

1. LIAMAE ETRARAH _____

2. ILOTP _____

3. PLAIRANE _____

4. TOREQUA _____

5. HANDLOW _____

Extension

What advances in navigation technology make what probably happened to Amelia Earhart and her navigator less likely to occur?

55. The Mystery of the Snake Charmer

In India, snake charmers perform on the streets, accompanied by a basket containing black nags—extremely poisonous Indian cobras. The snake charmer sits cross-legged on the ground, beside the basket, and begins to play a flute. As the snake charmer sways from side to side, the cobras rise from the basket, their forked tongues flickering. The cobras spread their hoods and sway from side to side, seeming to dance to the music. When the performer stops playing the flute, the cobras sink back into the basket.

How does the snake charmer cause cobras to sway and to appear to dance?

Lab: Nag-ging

In this lab, we'll examine the way your body reacts when your eyes are following a moving object.

Materials

Pencil

What to Do

1. Hold the pencil vertically (straight up) about 12 inches or so in front of your face.
2. Fix your eyes on the pencil and try not to blink.
3. Slowly move the pencil in a wide arc from side to side. Follow the moving pencil with your eyes, but without swiveling your neck. Pay attention to what happens to the rest of your body.

Describe Your Results

1. How does the pencil move?

   _____

2. How did your whole body move when you followed the moving pencil?

   _____

Snake Charmer (Continued)

What's the Solution?

Now that you have completed the lab, use what you discovered to solve "The Mystery of the Snake Charmer." Additional hints: Snakes are deaf and the eyes of a snake are always open. They do not have ears or eyelids. They also don't have necks, and cannot turn, or swivel, their heads.

Exercises

Fill in the blanks with the correct answer:

1. Indian snake charmers carry baskets containing very poisonous black _____, a type of cobra.

2. The _____ sits cross-legged on the ground next to the basket, and begins to play the flute.

3. As he plays, the snake charmer _____ from side to side.

4. The cobras rise from the basket, spread their _____, and sway from side to side.

5. The swaying cobras seem to _____ to the music.

True or False?

1. There are snake charmers who perform on the streets in India. _____

2. A black nag is a very poisonous kind of cobra. _____

3. When the snake charmer stops playing the flute, the cobras rise from the basket. _____

4. The cobra dances because it likes the flute music. _____

Unscramble these words from the activity:

1. OBRAC _____
2. KEANS MERCHAR _____
3. LUTEF _____
4. NECDA _____
5. OUSONSIOP _____

Extension

When a cobra sinks its fangs into a victim, why does it chew at the wound briefly before it pulls back its head?

56. The Mystery of the Abyss

The Abyss is a nickname for the Marianas Trench, which lies at the bottom of the Pacific Ocean south of the Philippines. The Marianas Trench is a huge hole in the ocean floor. It has the deepest bottom of all the earth's oceans and seas. Part of the Marianas Trench has a depth of 36,198 feet.

The ocean floor of the Abyss is in total darkness, with bone-crushing water pressure and near-freezing temperatures. There is almost no oxygen dissolved in the seawater at the bottom of the Abyss, and there are no green plants.

Despite these conditions there are microbes that live on the bottom of the deep trench, and some animal life—such as shrimp, scale worms, and sea cucumbers—live deep down in the Abyss as well.

How can any life survive deep down in the Marianas Trench?

Lab: Blackwater World

In this lab, we'll examine how very hot water from a hydrothermal vent mixes with surrounding water.

Materials

Soda straws	Aquarium tank
Two-hole rubber stopper	Food coloring
Scissors	Water
Clear glass bottle	About 18 inches of sturdy string

What to Do

1. Insert a soda straw into a hole in a two-hole rubber stopper.

2. Slide the straw down into the rubber stopper so that the end of the straw is flush with the bottom of the stopper.

3. Leave two inches or so of the straw extending up over the rubber stopper and use the scissors to cut away the rest of the straw.

4. Using your thumb and index finger, squeeze the top of the soda straw to make a narrow slit.

5. Push the other straw into the second hole in the stopper.

Abyss *(Continued)*

6. Slide the soda straw down through the rubber stopper until the top of the straw is level with the top of the stopper. Fit the rubber stopper with the straw into the neck of the glass bottle. The longer soda straw should extend downwards almost to the bottom of the bottle. Cut away the bottom of the longer soda straw as necessary to fit.

7. Tie one of the ends of the string around the neck of the bottle.

8. Fill the aquarium tank with very cold water.

9. Fill the bottle with very hot water and color it with food coloring.

10. Use the string to lower the bottle into the aquarium tank until the bottle is standing on the bottom. Observe for five minutes.

Describe Your Results

1. What happened when you first put the bottle of colored water on the bottom of the aquarium tank?

   _____

   _____

2. What did you observe a full five minutes after the bottle had been lowered to the bottom of the aquarium tank?

   _____

   _____

What's the Solution?

Now that you have completed the lab, use what you discovered to solve "The Mystery of the Abyss." Additional hint: The waters from hydrothermal vents also contain minerals that are important for life.

Exercises

Fill in the blanks with the correct answer:

1. The _____—also known as the Abyss—is at the bottom of the Pacific Ocean.

2. The Marianas Trench is a huge hole in the _____ floor.

Abyss *(Continued)*

3. There is a part of the Marianas Trench that is _____ feet deep.
4. The _____ of the Abyss has total darkness, crushing water pressure, and near-freezing temperatures.
5. The water at the bottom of the Abyss has hardly any _____ dissolved in it.

True or False?

1. The Marianas Trench is nicknamed the Black Hole.

   _____

2. The Marianas Trench is a huge hole in the bottom of the Pacific Ocean south of the Philippines. _____

3. Part of the Abyss (the Marianas Trench) is 36,198 feet deep.

   _____

4. The ocean floor of the Abyss has soft light and warm temperatures.

   _____

5. There is no life whatsoever on the bottom of the Marianas Trench (the Abyss). _____

Unscramble these words from the activity:

1. ARIMANSA THRENC _____
2. SYBAS _____
3. ALTOT NESSARKD _____
4. TERWA RESSUREP _____
5. GENOXY _____

Extension

Can you think of any practical use for hydrothermal vents and the super-heated water that seeps from them?

57. The Mystery of the Fejee Mermaid

The first tales of mermaids came from sailors who reported that they had seen these half-human, half-fish creatures while at sea. What sailors saw might have actually been dugongs or sea cows, which are relatives of the manatee, breaking through the surface of the ocean, perhaps to breathe. They may have had seaweed hanging from their heads that could have looked like the long hair of a woman.

In 1842, Phineas T. Barnum, the famous showman, exhibited in New York City something he called the Fejee Mermaid, which he claimed to be the body of a genuine mermaid. The Fejee Mermaid was a great sensation. Where could this mysterious creature have come from?

Lab: Frankenstein

In this lab, we'll create a creature from different parts.

Materials

Modeling clay

Fake fur pieces

Wool

Dried pig ears (sold as chews for dogs)

Feathers (such as from a feather duster)

Cleaned lobster or crab claws

Cleaned clam shells or other seashells

Scraps of leather

Paste or glue

Cellophane tape

What to Do

1. Lay the materials from the bodies of animals out on a table and study them.
2. Working as individuals or in groups, select items from the table and piece them together on a base of modeling clay to make new creatures.
3. Give your creature a name.

Fejee Mermaid *(Continued)*

Describe Your Results

1. Describe four of the body parts on the table.

   _____

   _____

2. On another sheet of paper, describe in detail the creature that you or your group designed. What does it eat? How does it find or catch food? How does it hide from predators?
3. List all of the body parts that were used to make your creature.

   _____

   _____

   _____

   _____

What's the Solution?

Now that you've completed the lab, use what you discovered to solve "The Mystery of the Fejee Mermaid."

Exercises

Fill in the blanks with the correct answer:

1. The first tales of mermaids came from _____.
2. These sailors may have actually seen _____, sea cows, breaking through the surface of the water.
3. Sea cows are relatives of the _____.
4. In _____, Phineas T. Barnum, the famous showman, exhibited the Fejee Mermaid in New York City.
5. The Fejee Mermaid was a great _____.

Fejee Mermaid *(Continued)*

True or False?

1. The first tales of mermaids came from gypsies, who reported that they had seen these creatures on big rocks by the sea.

   _____

2. People might have thought dugongs, or sea cows, were mermaids.

   _____

3. The manatee is a relative of the sea cow. _____

4. In 1842, Phineas T. Barnum exhibited what he called the Fejee Mermaid, which he claimed to be the body of a real mermaid.

   _____

5. The Fejee Mermaid raised very little public interest.

   _____

Unscramble these words from the activity:

1. EJEFE MADIERM _____
2. ARBMUN _____
3. LORIAS _____
4. GNOGDU _____
5. AMANEET _____

Extension

What was the Cardiff Giant, which was found buried in upper New York State?

58. The Mystery of Vermeer's Camera

The Dutch painter Jan Vermeer (1632–1675) was one of the greatest artists who ever lived. Vermeer's life and his paintings are mysterious. He created only about thirty paintings, had no protégés, or apprentices, and left no records. His images are so amazingly life-like that there has been speculation that he may have used a *camera obscura* (which means "dark room" in Latin) to help him in his work.

The camera obscura is the forerunner of the camera. It is an optical device that reproduces images like a camera, but instead of capturing them on film or digital memory, it projects them on a wall, or a screen. The images can then be traced and used as the basis for a painting.

Did Jan Vermeer, one of the world's greatest artists, use the camera obscura to create realistic paintings?

Lab: Look! A Pinhole Camera

In this lab, we'll examine how a pinhole camera, which is like a camera obscura, works.

Materials

Cardboard oatmeal container shaped like a cylinder

Fine sewing needle with a sharp point

Parchment or wax paper

Large rubber band

Good-sized candle and a candlestick holder

Matches (for adult use only)

What to Do

1. Use the needle to poke a tiny hole in the center of the bottom of an empty, cardboard oatmeal container that is shaped like a cylinder.

2. Make a drumhead by spreading parchment or wax paper over the open mouth of the container. Make the paper as smooth as is possible and secure it with a large rubber band.

3. Set the candle in the candlestick holder that is sitting on a table.

4. Have an adult light the candle.

5. Darken the room. The darker the better.

Vermeer's Camera *(Continued)*

6. Point the pinhole toward the lit candle, which should be about six inches away from the pinhole.

7. Look at the image of the candle flame on the paper drumhead, which is a screen.

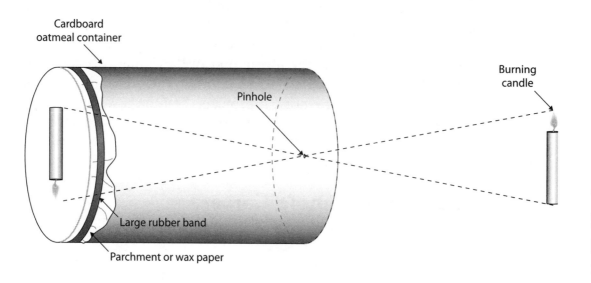

Cardboard oatmeal container

Pinhole

Burning candle

Large rubber band

Parchment or wax paper

Describe Your Results

1. What did you see on the paper drumhead?

_____

_____

2. How did the image of the candle compare to the original?

_____

_____

What's the Solution?

Now that you have completed the lab, use what you discovered to solve "The Mystery of Vermeer's Camera."

Vermeer's Camera *(Continued)*

Exercises

Fill in the blanks with the correct answer:

1. Jan Vermeer, the Dutch master, is one of the world's greatest
   _____.

2. Vermeer's paintings are amazingly _____.
3. There has been speculation that he may have used a camera
   _____ in his work.
4. The camera obscura is the forerunner of the _____.
5. The camera obscura is an optical device that reproduces
   _____ and projects them on a wall, or a screen,
   where they can be traced.

True or False?

1. Jan Vermeer was one of the world's greatest artists.
   _____

2. Vermeer had protégés, or apprentices, and created hundreds of
   paintings. _____
3. The camera obscura is the forerunner of the first camera.
   _____

4. The camera obscura projects images on a wall, or a screen, instead
   of capturing them on film or digital memory. _____
5. Jan Vermeer's paintings were not realistic.
   _____

Unscramble these words from the activity:

1. AMARCE RACUOBS _____
2. GHTIL _____
3. MAGEI _____
4. REVEERM _____
5. TIARST _____

Extension

Does the possibility that Jan Vermeer may have used a camera obscura to
trace images make the paintings that he created less important?

59. The Mystery of the Roswell Incident

On July 2, 1947, an explosion was heard during the night over Roswell, New Mexico, in America's southwest. The following day a rancher was riding in the desert on his horse when he saw broken pieces of shiny, silver metal scattered on the ground around him. The metal was not like any he had seen before. He stopped to pick up a piece, and found that it was extremely light in weight, could not be bent, and had some kind of picture writing—like ancient Egyptian hieroglyphics—on it. The rancher reported what he had found to the United States Air Force base in Roswell.

West of Roswell, an engineer working in the desert discovered a crash site. He claimed to have seen a big metal disc—a UFO (Unidentified Flying Object)—on the ground with five small bodies scattered around it. A military vehicle arrived at the scene, and the engineer was asked to leave and to talk to no one about what he had seen. Any debris from whatever had occurred was trucked away from the crash site by the air force.

Later, the U.S. Air Force reported that a weather balloon—which records the temperature and air pressure high in the sky—had crashed in the area, but many people were reluctant to believe this. They accused the U.S. government of covering up a real alien encounter and of hiding the spacecraft and bodies.

What really happened over Roswell?

Lab: Different Metals—Different Properties

In this lab, we'll observe what happens when two metals—aluminum and steel—are heated separately.

Materials

Two identical, empty glass wine bottles

One cork

A long aluminum knitting needle—the longer the better

One long steel knitting needle

Paper

Sewing needle

Glue

Good-sized candle

Match (for adult use only)

Roswell Incident *(Continued)*

What to Do

1. Make a paper arrow, or pointer, two inches long and three-eighths of an inch wide.

2. Fit the cork into the neck of one of the bottles.

3. Carefully push the point of the aluminum knitting needle into the side of the cork so that the needle extends away from the cork horizontally. The last inch or so of the needle should stretch across the mouth of the second bottle, which has no cork in it, and barely touch the bottle.

4. Push the sewing needle through the middle of the paper arrow so that the paper arrow is balanced on the needle.

5. Glue the arrow onto the sewing needle.

6. Slide the blunt end of the sewing needle under the part of the knitting needle that is sitting on the mouth of a bottle.

7. Set the arrow at a slant on the neck of the bottle.

8. Have an adult light the candle and place it so that the tip of its flame touches the middle of the knitting needle. Observe the paper arrow.

9. Repeat the activity; use a steel knitting needle instead of an aluminum knitting needle. Again observe the arrow.

Describe Your Results

1. What happened to the arrow when you heated the aluminum knitting needle?

   _____

   _____

2. What happened to the arrow when you used a steel knitting needle?

   _____

   _____

What's the Solution?

Now that you have completed the lab, use what you discovered to solve "The Mystery of the Roswell Incident." Additional hint: Weather balloons are made of tin foil, which bends easily.

Roswell Incident *(Continued)*

Exercises

Fill in the blanks with the correct answer:

1. On July 2, 1947, an _____ was heard over Roswell, New Mexico.
2. The following day, a _____ saw broken pieces of shiny, silver metal scattered on the ground.
3. The rancher reported what he found to the United States _____ base in Roswell.
4. An engineer who was working in the desert west of Roswell discovered a _____ site.
5. The U.S. Air Force reported that a _____ balloon had crashed in the area.

True or False?

1. On July 2, 1947, an explosion occurred over Roswell, New Mexico. _____

2. The next day, a rancher saw shiny, broken pieces of silver metal heaped neatly in a pile on the ground. _____
3. West of Roswell, an engineer discovered a crash site. _____

4. The engineer claimed to have seen a big metal disc and five small bodies on the ground. _____
5. The U.S. Air Force reported that an air force plane had crashed near Roswell. _____

Unscramble these words from the activity:

1. LEWORSL _____
2. EWN ICOEXM _____
3. RHACS TEIS _____
4. FUO _____
5. EATWREH NOLOBLA _____

Extension

Find out more about the latest advances in metals and how the new metals are used. Do the metals supposedly found at Roswell seem like any of those?

60. The Mystery of the War That Never Happened

Jean Eugene Robert-Houdin was a great French magician whose knowledge of science—especially electricity—helped him greatly in mystifying people with his magic feats. But what is most amazing is that it also helped him prevent a war.

In 1856, the government of France asked Robert-Houdin to go to Algeria, then a colony of France in northern Africa, where it was feared that the people were being encouraged by religious leaders to overthrow the rule of France. These religious leaders were supposedly performing "miracles" to support their cause. Later that year, Robert-Houdin appeared on a stage in Algeria and presented his magic to an audience of Algerian leaders to demonstrate his power and the power of France.

One of the effects that he presented involved a small chest that a strong, muscular man from the audience was able to lift easily. When Robert-Houdin then told the man that he, the volunteer, was now weak and could not lift the chest, the brawny man tried—and struggled—to pick up the chest but could not do so. This plus other effects convinced the Algerians that the French were more powerful than the religious leaders, and the threat of war disappeared. A magician had stopped a war before it began.

How did Robert-Houdin control the chest so that it could not be lifted?

Lab: On Again, Off Again

In this lab, we'll examine how an electric current can be used to make a type of magnet called an electromagnet.

Materials

Iron bolt, preferably a soft iron bolt (A soft iron bolt is made of cast iron, which loses its magnetism when the electrical current is switched off. A steel bolt retains its magnetism for a while when the current electricity stops flowing.)

One or two yards of insulated copper wire

Steel-jacketed, dry-cell battery (1.5 volts)

Masking tape or cellophane tape

Metal paper clips

Thumbtacks

Nails

War That Never Happened (Continued)

What to Do

1. Coil the wire around the iron bolt.

2. Have an adult carefully strip one-half inch of insulation off each of the ends of the wire to expose the bare wire.

3. Connect the bare ends of the wire to the battery. Use masking tape, or cellophane tape, to attach one end of the wire to the battery's terminal, which is a button on top of the battery. The other end of the wire must be attached with tape to the steel side of the battery.

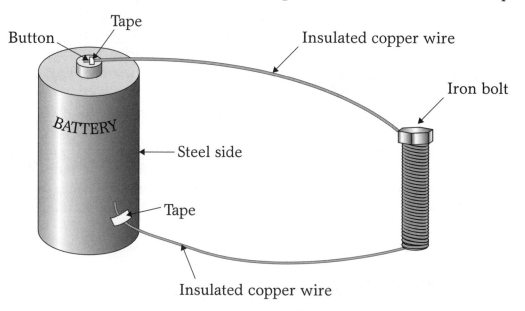

4. Hold the bolt close to some things that contain iron, such as paper clips, thumbtacks, and nails. Observe.

5. Disconnect the wire from the battery and again hold the bolt close to the metal objects. Observe.

Describe Your Results

1. What happened when the wire coil and the iron bolt were connected to the dry-cell battery and you brought the bolt near things that contain iron?

   _____

   _____

2. What happened when the wire coil and the iron bolt were disconnected from the dry-cell battery and you brought the bolt near things that contain iron?

   _____

   _____

War That Never Happened *(Continued)*

What's the Solution?

Now that you have completed the lab, use what you discovered to solve "The Mystery of the War That Never Happened." Additional hint: There was an iron plate in the bottom of Robert-Houdin's magic chest.

Exercises

Fill in the blanks with the correct answer:

1. Robert-Houdin was a great _____.
2. Robert-Houdin had knowledge of science, especially _____, which was useful to him as a magician.
3. In 1856, Robert-Houdin was asked by the French government to go to _____, then a French colony in northern Africa.
4. Robert-Houdin appeared on _____ before the Algerian leaders.
5. One of Robert-Houdin's acts involved making a small _____ impossible to lift.

True or False?

1. Robert-Houdin was a great British magician. _____
2. Robert-Houdin's knowledge of science was helpful in his work as a magician. _____
3. Robert-Houdin's skills as a magician helped him to prevent a war. _____
4. The French government asked Robert-Houdin to travel to Algeria because it was feared that the Algerian people were being urged to overthrow the rule of France. _____
5. Robert-Houdin's magic convinced the Algerian leaders that they must overthrow the rule of France. _____

Unscramble these words from the activity:

1. GNAMET _____
2. CEETRICLYTI _____
3. GNATROCELEEMT _____
4. ONRI LBOT _____
5. GIAMACNI _____

Extension

Find out how an electric doorbell works. How does it relate to the electromagnet you made?

189

61. The Mystery of the Floating Island

There is a famous island in Derwentwater, England, that usually, but not always, appears in a lake in the summer and remains for a few weeks before disappearing again. The island always appears in the same place.

The island is solid and firm. In fact, the town band from Keswick landed on it on one occasion and presented a concert. The island consists mainly of peat, or sod, and it rises and falls with the level of the lake's water.

How is it possible that the island appears, remains for a few weeks, and then disappears?

Lab: Going Up—Going Down

In this lab, we'll examine how something can be made to rise and fall in water.

Materials

Glass jar	2 tablespoons of baking soda
Water	4 tablespoons of vinegar
Teaspoon	Mothballs

What to Do

1. Fill the glass jar with water.
2. Add baking soda to the water and stir.
3. Add vinegar to the water.
4. Carefully drop a few mothballs into the water. Observe.

Describe Your Results

1. What happened when you added vinegar to the mixture of water and baking soda?

_____

_____

Floating Island *(Continued)*

2. What happened when you first dropped mothballs into the jar?

   _____

   _____

3. What happened after the mothballs had been in the jar for a few minutes?

   _____

   _____

4. What happened to each mothball when it rose to the surface of the water?

   _____

   _____

What's the Solution?

Now that you have completed the lab, use what you discovered to solve "The Mystery of the Floating Island." Additional hint: Decaying plants give off gases.

Exercises

Fill in the blanks with the correct answer:

1. There is a famous island in Derwentwater, _____, that appears in the summer.
2. When the island appears, it usually remains on the surface for a few _____ and then disappears.
3. The island always appears in the _____ place in the lake.
4. The island is solid and _____.
5. A town _____ landed on the island on one occasion and held a concert.

Floating Island (Continued)

True or False?

1. There is a well-known island in Derwentwater, England.

   _____

2. The island appears in a lake in the fall and disappears in the spring.

   _____

3. The island never appears in the same place. _____

4. The island is made mainly of peat. _____

5. The island rises and falls with the level of the lake water.

   _____

Unscramble these words from the activity:

1. SLADIN _____
2. LFOATNGI _____
3. KEAL _____
4. AGS _____
5. ATEP _____

Extension

Find out more about methane, the type of gas that forms in marshes.

62. The Mystery of the Disappearing Planet

In 1860, M. Lescarbault, a French physician, reported that he had observed a large black circle, which he believed to be a new planet, move across the upper part of the sun's face. Urbain Jean Joseph Leverrier, a world-famous astronomer who was the director of the Observatory of Paris, verified Lescarbault's discovery, and calculated the new planet's mean distance from the sun to be about 13 million miles, and for its period of revolution 19 days 17 hours. Leverrier verified Lescarbault's discovery by calculation, not by actual observation. Lescarbault named the planet Vulcan. Others challenged the existence of Vulcan. They attempted to locate the planet and track its movement without success. It was as though the planet had vanished.

By 1878, astronomers agreed that a major mistake had been made. The planet did not exist. Vulcan disappeared from the list of known planets, which at that time included Mercury, Venus, Earth, Mars, the Asteroid Belt, Jupiter, Saturn, Uranus, and Neptune. Pluto was discovered in 1930.

What did M. Lescarbault see?

Lab: Now You See It, Now You Don't (Teacher Demonstration)

In this lab, we'll examine what can be seen crossing the path of the sun by observing its image as projected through binoculars.

Materials

Pair of binoculars (6X magnification is excellent)

Mirror with a stand (such as a shaving mirror)

What to Do

Warning: NEVER LOOK DIRECTLY AT THE SUN. LOOKING DIRECTLY AT THE SUN CAN CAUSE SERIOUS EYE INJURY—EVEN BLINDNESS.

1. On a sunny day, open a window wide.
2. Position the binoculars on the windowsill so that the objective lenses—the big lenses of the binoculars—point toward the sun like twin telescopes. Use heavy books to support the binoculars.

Disappearing Planet *(Continued)*

3. Stand the mirror on the sill in front of one of the eyepieces (the smaller lenses) so that an image of the sun is reflected off the mirror and projected onto the opposite wall.

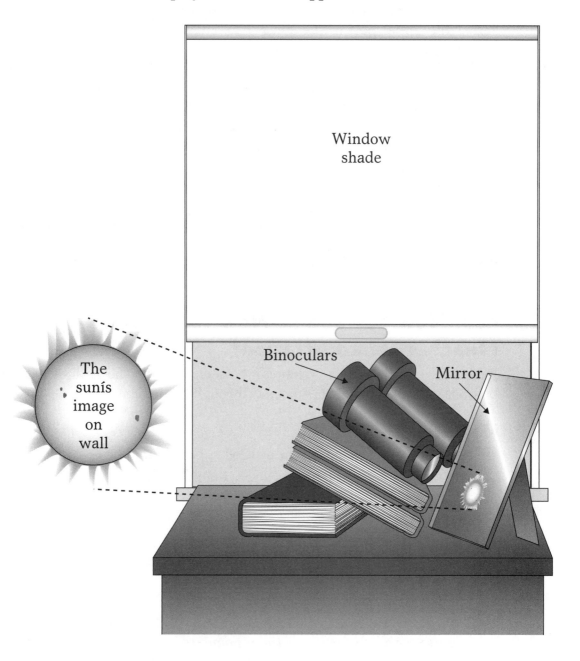

Disappearing Planet *(Continued)*

4. Darken the room and adjust the mirror to sharpen the image.

5. Study the image of the sun projected on the wall.

6. Adjust the position of the binoculars as necessary so that they continue to point to the sun as it moves. (The rotation of the earth causes the sun's image to move across the wall rather quickly.)

Describe Your Results

1. What did you see on the wall when the binoculars were pointed at the sun?

   _____

   _____

2. Give details of any black spots or shadows you could see on the sun's image.

   _____

   _____

3. Describe the movement of the circle of light across the wall.

   _____

   _____

What's the Solution?

Now that you have completed the lab, use what you discovered to solve "The Mystery of the Disappearing Planet." Additional hint: A sunspot is a dark spot on the sun's surface that is cooler than the surrounding area.

Exercises

Fill in the blanks with the correct answer:

1. In 1860, M. Lescarbault reported that he had observed a large _____ circle move across the face of the sun.

2. Lescarbault named the new planet _____.

3. Others attempted to _____ the planet and track its movement.

Disappearing Planet (Continued)

4. By the year _____, astronomers agreed that a mistake had been made.

5. The planet _____ was discovered in 1930.

True or False?

1. In 1860, M. Lescarbault reported that he had observed a big, black circle move across the sun's face. _____

2. Many astronomers verified M. Lescarbault's belief that he had discovered a new planet. _____

3. M. Lescarbault named the new planet Vulcan. _____

4. M. Lescarbault had actually discovered Pluto. _____

5. By 1878, astronomers agreed that the planet Vulcan did not exist. _____

Unscramble these words from the activity:

1. ESLCARLTAUB _____
2. TENLAP _____
3. ERASTRMONO _____
4. LUVNAC _____
5. SNUSTOP _____

Extension

Is it likely that any additional planets will be discovered in our solar system?

63. The Mystery of the *Titanic*

Shortly before midnight on April 14, 1912, the British luxury liner, *Titanic,* which was at the time the biggest ship in the world and believed by many people to be unsinkable, hit an iceberg and quickly sank about 400 miles south of Newfoundland.

An iceberg is a huge mass of ice that has broken away from a glacier and floats in the ocean. A glacier is a field of ice, an ice sheet, that is formed by compacted (packed tightly together) snow, and moves or flows because of gravity.

The *Titanic's* hull was built around a series of separate watertight compartments, which had automatic doors that could be sealed off from one another when there was any damage to the hull. It was believed that, even if the *Titanic* did hit an iceberg and the ship experienced damage, the ship's compartments would limit the flooding of the ship, and the ship would remain afloat. Amazingly, six small cuts below the *Titanic's* waterline were sufficient to sink what was the biggest ship in the world.

When the *Titanic* struck the iceberg, the first five compartments in the forward part of the *Titanic* filled with seawater. The weight of the water pushed the ship's bow down so that water overtopped the compartments, and filled the sixth compartment. Water overtopped the sixth compartment and filled the seventh compartment. This cycle continued one compartment after another until the whole ship sank.

Why couldn't the crew of the *Titanic* see the huge iceberg and turn the ship to avoid hitting it?

Lab: Brrrrrr!

In this lab, we'll examine what happens when water freezes and how ice floats in water.

Materials

Ice cube tray	Freezer
Water	Drinking glass
Ruler	Plate

What to Do

1. Fill an ice cube tray halfway up with water.
2. Use a ruler to measure the distance from the surface of the water to the top of the tray.

Titanic *(Continued)*

3. Put the tray in the freezer.

4. When the cubes are frozen, measure the distance from the top surfaces of the ice cubes to the top of the tray.

5. Put the glass on the plate and put an ice cube into the glass.

6. Carefully fill the glass with water up to its rim. Observe what happens.

7. Allow the ice cube to melt for three full minutes in the water. Observe.

Describe Your Results

1. Note the measurements you took in steps 2 and 4. Was there any difference between the height from the water in the ice cube tray to the top of the tray and the height from the ice cubes in the tray to the top of the tray?

   _____

   _____

2. What happened when an ice cube was placed in the glass and the glass was filled to the rim with water?

   _____

   _____

3. How much of the floating ice cube was above the surface of the water and how much was below the surface of the water?

   _____

   _____

4. What happened when you allowed the ice cube to melt?

   _____

   _____

What's the Solution?

Now that you have completed the lab, use what you discovered to solve "The Mystery of the *Titanic.*"

Titanic (Continued)

Exercises

Fill in the blanks with the correct answer:

1. On April 14, 1912, the _____, the biggest ship in the world, hit an iceberg.

2. Many people believed that the *Titanic* was _____, and would not sink even if it *did* hit an iceberg.

3. An iceberg is a huge mass of ice that has broken away from a _____.

4. A glacier is a field of ice that is formed by compacted (packed tightly together) _____, and moves or flows.

5. Six small _____ below the *Titanic*'s waterline were enough to sink the big luxury liner.

True or False?

1. The *Titanic* was a medium-sized cargo ship. _____

2. Many people believed that the *Titanic* was unsinkable. _____

3. The *Titanic* hit an iceberg, and quickly sank about 400 miles south of Newfoundland. _____

4. The *Titanic* sank on a sunny afternoon. _____

5. An iceberg is a huge mass of rock that is covered with snow and floats in the ocean. _____

Unscramble these words from the activity:

1. ICTANIT _____
2. CEIERGB _____
3. RIECGLA _____
4. EIC _____
5. STOAFL _____

Extension

How do new technologies plus other developments since 1912 make the icebergs in the North Atlantic less of a problem for ships at sea today?

64. The Mystery of the Little Georgia Magnet

Annie Abbott was an American entertainer who, during the late 1800s, claimed to be a human magnet, a person who has unique magnetic power.

In her performance, the "Little Georgia Magnet" grasped the hand of a little girl or boy and stared into the child's eyes intently. She then announced to the spectators that she had transferred magnetic power to the child, and that a strong man would be unable to lift the child by the elbows up off the floor.

A strong man from the audience joined the performer and tried to lift the child by the elbows up off the floor. Invariably, the man was unable to do so.

Also in her act, Annie Abbott would hold a long, slender rod in front of her, with both hands, and ask some men in the audience to join her on stage. Annie Abbott challenged the volunteers to push her backwards by all of them gripping the horizontal rod with both hands and pressing the rod forward with force. All of the men together were unable to push Annie backwards.

How was Annie Abbott, the "Little Georgia Magnet," able to do these things?

Lab: The Force Is with You

In this lab, we'll examine center of gravity and the absorption of force.

What to Do

Activity 1
1. Ask a friend to sit on a chair. Your friend's back must be straight so that his or her chin is up and head is back.
2. Place your index finger or your forefinger on your friend's forehead and press.
3. Ask your friend to stand up. Observe.

Little Georgia Magnet (Continued)

Activity 2

1. Place the palms of your hands against a wall with your fingers pointing up toward the ceiling. Your arms should be outstretched. Stiffen your arms and brace yourself.

2. Ask a few students to line up in back of you and have each of the students place both hands on the shoulders of the student in front of him or her. If possible, put the person you think has the least strength in the position right in back of you.

3. At your signal, everyone should push with all of his or her strength and try to push you against the wall.

Describe Your Results

1. What happened when you placed your finger on your friend's forehead and asked your friend to stand up?

   _____

   _____

2. What happened when the line of students tried to push you against the wall?

   _____

   _____

What's the Solution?

Now that you have completed the lab, use what you discovered to solve "The Mystery of the Little Georgia Magnet."

Exercises

Fill in the blanks with the correct answer:

1. Annie Abbott was called the Little _____ Magnet.

2. In her show, she stared into the _____ of a child intently and announced that she had transferred magnetic power to the child.

3. A strong man from the audience tried to lift the child by the _____ .

Little Georgia Magnet *(Continued)*

4. Annie would also hold a long, slender rod in front of her with both hands, and ask volunteers to press the rod forward all together and try to push her _____.

5. All of the men together at the same time were _____ to push Annie Abbott backwards.

True or False?

1. Annie Abbott was an American entertainer who claimed to be a human magnet. _____

2. In her show, the "Little Georgia Magnet" announced that a child had transferred magnetic power to her. _____

3. A strong man from the audience tried to lift the child by the elbows, but was unable to do so. _____

4. In her act, Annie Abbott held a long rod horizontally in front of her and asked men from the audience to grip the rod with both hands all together. _____

5. The men pushed the rod forward all together and the "Little Georgia Magnet" fell backwards. _____

Unscramble these words from the activity:

1. NIANE TBOTAB _____
2. ERNTRASF _____
3. NEMAGCIT WROEP _____
4. LFTI _____
5. TILETL GRIAGEO NAGTEM _____

Extension

Why must gymnasts understand center of gravity and how levers work?

65. The Mystery of the Firewalkers

Firewalkers are people who can walk barefoot over heated stones without feeling pain or injuring their feet. The stones usually are spread outdoors on a bed of burning bundles of wood in a shallow pit dug in the ground. Firewalkers perform in the Fiji Islands, on the islands of Tahiti, Mauritius, and Trinidad, and in India and Japan.

How is it possible for firewalkers to walk barefoot over heated stones without pain or injury?

Lab: Hot Stuff!

In this lab, we'll examine objects that glow without giving off much heat.

Materials

Glow stick, glow necklace, or glow bracelet

Fluorescent lamp

What to Do

1. Darken the room.
2. Activate the glow stick, necklace, or bracelet. Observe.
3. Feel the glow stick, necklace, or bracelet with your fingers.
4. Have your teacher switch on the fluorescent lamp. After three or four minutes have elapsed, feel the glowing tube with your fingers.

Describe Your Results

1. What happened when you activated the glow stick, necklace, or bracelet in the darkened room?

   _____

   _____

2. What did the glow stick, necklace, or bracelet feel like?

   _____

   _____

Firewalkers *(Continued)*

3. What did the fluorescent lamp feel like?

_____

_____

What's the Solution?

Now that you have completed the lab, use what you discovered to solve "The Mystery of the Firewalkers."

Exercises

Fill in the blanks with the correct answer:

1. Firewalkers are people who have the ability to walk _____ over heated stones.

2. Firewalkers do not feel _____ when they walk over the stones.

3. The stones are spread on a bed of _____ bundles of wood in a shallow pit.

4. Firewalkers perform in the Fiji Islands and on the islands of _____, Mauritius, and Trinidad.

5. Firewalkers also perform in _____ and Japan.

True or False?

1. Firewalkers do not feel pain or injure their feet when they walk barefoot over heated stones. _____

2. The stones are spread over a bed of bundles of wood that are burning in a shallow pit. _____

3. Firewalkers wear heavy leather sandals when they walk on heated stones. _____

4. Firewalkers perform in the Fiji Islands and on the island of Tahiti.

5. There are firewalkers in Egypt and in China as well.

_____

Firewalkers (Continued)

Unscramble these words from the activity:

1. REFIWAKLSRE _____
2. EDHETA TSONSE _____
3. HSALLWO TPI _____
4. REIF _____
5. REBATOOF _____

Extension

Do you think that firewalkers could also walk barefoot on a sheet of ice without injury?

66. The Mystery of the Human Fly

It was October 7, 1916. A huge crowd of 150,000 people had gathered on the sidewalks and in the streets of a big intersection in downtown Detroit, Michigan. Traffic had stopped completely in the sea of people.

The enormous crowd had gathered to see Harry H. Gardiner, the man whom President Grover Cleveland had named "The Human Fly," climb the face of the fourteen-story Majestic Building. In 1916, this handsome building was considered a skyscraper.

Harry H. Gardiner was dressed in a white suit and was wearing a white hat and white tennis shoes. Hand over hand, and foothold over foothold, the Human Fly climbed up over the bricks and the big stone blocks of the tall building. It was thirty-seven minutes later when Harry H. Gardiner completed his climb of 211 feet. He waved to the cheering crowd from the top of the building.

Many years later, on May 25, 1981, Daniel Goodwin, who was also a human fly, climbed 1,454 feet up the 110-story Sears Tower in Chicago, Illinois. He was dressed like Spider-man. How were these daring men able to climb up the sheer faces of buildings with no ropes?

Lab: Things Are Looking Up

In this lab, we'll see whether we can make a stuffed animal hang from a wall like a human fly.

Materials

Small stuffed animal

Suction cups

Alligator clips (An alligator clip is a metal clip that has a hinged jaw with teeth and moves like an alligator's jaw. Alligator clips are usually used to connect electrical components. They are available at electronics supply stores.)

Rubber bands

Twist ties

Cellophane tape

Human Fly *(Continued)*

What to Do

1. Attach the suction cups and the alligator clips to the small toy stuffed animal. Use rubber bands, or other twist ties, and cellophane tape as needed.
2. Attach the toy stuffed animal to a wall. Use the suction cups and the alligator clips to anchor the toy animal to the wall so that it looks like it is climbing.

Describe Your Results

1. What did you attach to the small toy stuffed animal?

   _____

   _____

2. How did you attach the toy stuffed animal to a wall to make the toy animal look like it was climbing?

   _____

   _____

What's the Solution?

Now that you have completed the lab, use what you discovered to solve "The Mystery of the Human Fly." Additional hint: Harry H. Gardiner did not have suction cups or alligator clips, but he did wear tennis shoes.

Exercises

Fill in the blanks with the correct answer:

1. President Grover Cleveland named Harry H. Gardiner "The Human _____."
2. On October 7, 1916, a crowd of 150,000 people gathered in downtown _____, Michigan, to see the Human Fly.
3. Harry H. Gardiner climbed the face of the fourteen-story _____ Building.

Human Fly *(Continued)*

4. In thirty-seven minutes, he completed his climb of _____ feet, and the crowd cheered.

5. On May 25, 1981, Daniel Goodwin climbed 1,454 feet up the _____ Tower in Chicago.

True or False?

1. On October 7, 1916, 150,000 people gathered in Detroit, Michigan, to see Harry H. Gardiner climb the face of a tall building.

   _____

2. It was President Woodrow Wilson who named Harry H. Gardiner "The Human Fly." _____

3. The Human Fly climbed 211 feet to the top of the Majestic Building and waved to the cheering crowd. _____

4. Daniel Goodwin climbed the Sears Tower dressed as Batman.

   _____

Unscramble these words from the activity:

1. UHNAM FYL _____
2. CITJESMA UBILDGIN _____
3. YSKSCRPAER _____
4. CIMLB _____
5. DOWCR _____

Extension

Would it be easier, or more difficult, for a human fly to climb down the face of a tall building than up? Why?

67. The Mystery of the Mummy's Curse

King Tutankhamen was a pharaoh of ancient Egypt. When he died, his remains were mummified and laid to rest in a grand tomb. The rooms of King Tut's burial site were built underground and carved out of stone. The site has a burial chamber where Tut's mummy was found, plus three other rooms that were filled with things that he believed he would need in the afterlife, including 116 baskets of fruit, wooden boxes containing a variety of meats and other foods, as well as his gold and silver throne, four chariots, weapons, clothing, and jewelry.

It was said that a curse had been placed on King Tut's burial site, and that evil would come to anyone who entered his tomb.

The curse seemed to come true soon after British archaeologist, Howard Carter, discovered and entered the burial site in 1922. Howard Carter's associate, Lord Carnarvon, the Egyptologist who helped to finance the excavations that led to the discovery of Tut's tomb, died from a mosquito bite that became infected. It is said that when Lord Carnarvon died, all of the lights in the city of Cairo, Egypt, went dark, and Lord Carnarvon's dog began to howl and then died.

Other tragic events followed. Records show that during the 1920s more than two dozen people who had entered King Tut's tomb died soon after.

Is it possible that the mummy's curse was real?

Lab: Strange Things Are Happening!

In this lab, we'll examine how molds grow in warm, dark places. (**Caution:** Do not perform this lab if you are allergic to molds.)

Materials

Orange (The orange must have a spot of green mold on it!)

Slice of blue cheese or Roquefort cheese (These cheeses have mold in them.)

Slice of bread (White bread works best because any change that takes place in the bread can be readily seen.)

Three clear glass jars

Water

Mummy's Curse *(Continued)*

What to Do

1. Wet the orange and slip it into a clear glass jar.
2. Moisten the piece of cheese and drop it into another clear glass jar.
3. Wet your fingertips and shake a few drops of water onto the slice of bread. Slide the bread into a third clear glass jar.
4. Put all three jars in a warm, dark place.
5. Look at the orange, the cheese, and the bread every day for at least fourteen days, and see whether there are any changes.

Describe Your Results

1. What happened to the orange?

   _____

   _____

2. What happened to the cheese?

   _____

   _____

3. What happened to the slice of bread?

   _____

   _____

What's the Solution?

Now that you have completed the lab, use what you discovered to solve "The Mystery of the Mummy's Curse." Additional hints: Some reports say that a black fungus was found inside Tut's tomb. Some people are highly allergic to molds.

Exercises

Fill in the blanks with the correct answer:

1. Tutankhamen was a pharaoh of ancient _____.
2. When King Tut _____, his remains were mummified.

Mummy's Curse *(Continued)*

3. It was said that a curse had been placed on Tut's _____ site.

4. It was also said that _____ would come to anybody who entered the King's tomb.

5. Soon after the burial site was discovered in _____, tragic things began to happen to people who had entered the tomb.

True or False?

1. It was said that good luck would come to anyone who entered King Tut's tomb. _____

2. Howard Carter, a British archaeologist, discovered Tut's burial site in 1922. _____

3. When Lord Carnarvon, who was Howard Carter's associate, died, it is said that all of the lights in Cairo, Egypt, went dark.

_____

4. During the 1920s, more than two dozen people who had entered the tomb died. _____

5. The walls of Tutankhamen's burial site were built out of wood and stood in the open desert. _____

Unscramble these words from the activity:

1. RACHEOISATLOG _____
2. MBOT _____
3. MYUMM _____
4. SECUR _____
5. CROAI _____

Extension

Another mold was discovered in the 1920s, but this one has saved many lives. Find out more about the discovery of penicillin.

68. The Mystery of the Floating Lights

There are places where mysterious glowing lights reportedly can be seen floating over the ground when it is dark. The lights seem to glide like ghosts through the blackness of the night, and then vanish. These lights have been observed in places that also have mysterious stone monuments, including Stonehenge in England, Harold's Stones in Wales, and Carnac in France. Scientists have found that their readings of the levels of electromagnetic energy in these places are very different from the levels of electromagnetic energy found elsewhere.

The mysterious, glowing lights that float like ghosts in the dark continue to be a mystery. What are these strange lights, and what causes them?

Lab: Crunch!

In this lab, we'll observe what happens when a crystal sugar tablet is broken into two pieces in a dark room.

Materials

Crystal sugar tablet (Do not use a sugar cube. Tablets are larger and easier to break. A Necco candy wafer can be used instead of a crystal sugar tablet.)

What to Do

1. Pick up the crystal sugar tablet or the Necco candy wafer.
2. Darken the room—the darker the better.
3. With your fingers and thumbs, break the crystal sugar tablet or the candy wafer into two pieces. Observe what occurs.

What's the Solution?

Now that you have completed the lab, use what you discovered to solve "The Mystery of the Floating Lights."

Floating Lights (Continued)

Exercises

Fill in the blanks with the correct answer:

1. There are places where mysterious _____ seem to glide above the ground through the night air.
2. Floating lights reportedly have been seen in places where there are also mysterious stone _____.
3. Stone monuments include Stonehenge in England, Harold's Stones in Wales, and _____ in France.
4. Areas around the stones have unusual levels of electromagnetic _____.

True or False?

1. Floating lights have been observed at Stonehenge in England and in other places that have mysterious stone monuments.
   _____
2. Stonehenge, Harold's Stones, and Carnac are the names of famous resorts. _____
3. There is no electromagnetic energy in the places where floating lights reportedly have been seen. _____

Unscramble these words from the activity:

1. GNIOATFL TSLIGH _____
2. ONSTEHENEG _____
3. ETONS MUONMENST _____
4. NRACCA _____
5. EELTROCGAMNETCI ERENGY _____

Extension

Find out about living things that glow in the dark. How do they make light?

69. The Mystery of the Giant Squid

Tales of giant squids roaming the oceans and frightening sailors have been around for hundreds of years. But many people disbelieved that such creatures could exist, and the sailors had no physical evidence as proof. On November 30, 1861, a French steamship, the *Alecton,* looped a steel cable around a giant squid, which had surfaced off the Canary Islands. The cable dug deeply into the squid, and a big part of its body broke off as the huge creature slipped back into the sea. The body part was sent to the French Academy of the Sciences, which reported that the find was a fraud. The French academy reported that no such creature could exist.

On November 2, 1878, three fishermen discovered a giant squid that was stuck, but still alive, in shallow water. When the tide receded, the squid was left behind and died. The creature measured 20 feet from the tail to the beak, or mouth. The two longest arms or tentacles were 35 feet long, with four-inch suction cups.

The reason we rarely see giant squids is that they live deep down in the open ocean at depths of 700 to 3,300 feet. They can even live at depths as great as 13,300 feet.

Like all squids, a giant squid has five pairs of arms. One pair of tentacles is longer and is used to catch food and bring it to the creature's beak, or mouth. The beak is powerful enough to cut through a steel cable. The eyes of a giant squid are like human eyes, but are up to 18 inches in diameter. Some believe that giant squids can be as much as 75 feet long and weigh up to 1,000 pounds.

Why are these giant creatures able to live deep in the ocean where the pressure would crush a human, but unable to live in warm shallow waters?

Lab: Deep Water

In this lab, we'll examine differences in water pressure at different depths. We'll also see how pressure affects gas in a solution.

Giant Squid *(Continued)*

Materials

Clean, empty 1-quart milk carton

Dishpan

Tap water

Unopened clear bottle of soda

Bottle opener

What to Do

Activity 1

1. Punch three holes vertically in the side of the milk carton. The holes should be the same size and an equal distance apart.

2. Set the milk carton in the dishpan.

3. Fill the milk carton with water up to a level just below the lip, or opening. Observe what happens.

Activity 2

1. Remove the bottle cap from the bottle of soda. Observe what happens.

2. Leave the bottle open for ten full minutes and note any changes after that time.

3. Leave the bottle open for another ten minutes. Again, observe any changes.

Describe Your Results

1. In Activity 1, what happened when the milk carton with three holes in it was filled with water? What was the difference between the three streams of water from the three holes?

   _____

   _____

2. In Activity 2, describe the appearance of the soda in the bottle before the bottle cap was removed.

   _____

   _____

Giant Squid *(Continued)*

3. What happened to the soda when the bottle cap was removed?

_____

_____

4. Describe the appearance of the soda after the bottle had been left open for ten minutes.

_____

_____

5. Describe the appearance of the soda after an additional ten minutes had elapsed.

_____

_____

What's the Solution?

Now that you have completed your lab, use what you discovered to solve "The Mystery of the Giant Squid." Additional hint: See Activity 3, "The Mystery of the Brooklyn Bridge Disease."

Exercises

Fill in the blanks with the correct answer:

1. In 1861, the *Alecton,* a French steamship, looped a steel cable around a giant _____.

2. There are those who believe that giant squids can grow to a length of as much as _____ feet and weigh up to 1,000 pounds.

3. The longest tentacles of the squid are used to _____ food.

4. A giant squid's eyes are like human eyes but can be up to _____ inches in diameter.

5. Giant squids live deep down in the open ocean and are rarely seen in warmer, _____ waters.

Hands-On Science Mysteries for Grades 3–6

Giant Squid *(Continued)*

True or False?

1. Giant squids live in the open ocean at depths that range from 700 feet to thousands of feet. _____

2. Giant squids are almost never seen in warmer, shallower ocean waters. _____

3. A giant squid's beak can cut through a steel cable. _____

4. Giant squids do not exist. _____

5. Giant squids prefer warm, shallow ocean waters. _____

Unscramble these words from the activity:

1. GINAT IDQUS _____
2. ESTATENCL _____
3. OWALLSH ERTWA _____
4. EAOCN _____
5. KEBA _____

Extension

What might cause a giant squid to come up and be seen near the ocean's surface?

70. The Mystery of the Singing Statue

A pair of gigantic statues stands in the desert west of the Nile River in Egypt. The statues are made of quartzite and depict the Egyptian pharaoh, or king, Amenophis III, who lived almost 3,500 years ago. The statues are called the Colossi of Memnon. Each of the statues stands about 60 feet tall and weighs about 1,000 tons. The faces and the tall crowns are missing from the statues. In ancient times, the pair of colossi guarded the entry to a large temple, which no longer exists.

An earthquake damaged the statues in 27 B.C., and the colossus to the north lost the upper part of its torso. After the earthquake, this badly damaged statue made mysterious sounds—always at sunrise—sounds that were said to be musical.

The Greeks named the singing colossus The Oracle of Memnon because they believed the statue was speaking for the Greek god of that name. In 199 A.D., the Roman emperor Septimius Severus had the statues repaired. Ever since, the statue has been silent.

What caused the mysterious singing of the Colossus of Memnon?

Lab: Listen!

Sounds are caused by objects vibrating. In this lab, we'll examine how sounds can be produced in stone and glass by temperature changes and friction.

Materials

Piece of flint (The flint should be the size of an ice cube or bigger. Flint is available at scientific supply houses.)

Water

Tea kettle	Empty coffee can
Safety goggles	Wine glass with thin walls
Dishpan	One teaspoonful of vinegar

What to Do

Activity 1 (Teacher demonstration)

1. Chill the flint in a refrigerator freezer for 24 hours.

2. Put the water in the kettle and heat it to boiling.

3. The teacher should put on the safety glasses and make sure that the students are well away from the demonstration table.

4. Put the dishpan on the table.

Singing Statue (Continued)

5. Place the empty coffee can upside down in the dishpan.
6. Remove the thoroughly chilled flint from the freezer.
7. Position the flint on top of the can.
8. Pour the boiling water onto the flint. Observe and listen.

Activity 2

1. Pour water into the wine glass until the glass is half full.
2. Dip your forefinger into the water, and then slide the tip of your finger slowly around the rim of the glass. Do this until you get the glass to make a sound. (Note: If you dip your fingertip into a little vinegar instead of the water, the result may be better.)
3. Listen to the sound and observe the surface of the water.

Describe Your Results

1. In Activity 1, what did you observe while boiling water was being poured onto the chilled flint?

   _____

   _____

2. Describe any sounds that you heard.

   _____

   _____

3. In Activity 2, what happened when you slid the tip of your finger slowly around the rim of the glass?

   _____

   _____

What's the Solution?

Now that you have completed your lab, use what you discovered to solve "The Mystery of the Singing Statue." Additional hints: Cold makes things contract. Heat makes things expand. Temperatures in the desert go from very cold at night to very hot during the day quite quickly.

Singing Statue *(Continued)*

Exercises

Fill in the blanks with the correct answer:

1. In Egypt, a pair of gigantic _____ stand in the desert west of the Nile River.

2. Each of the gigantic statues is about 60 feet tall and _____ about 1,000 tons.

3. An _____ damaged the colossi in 27 B.C., and one statue lost much of its torso.

4. After the earthquake, the statue that had been badly damaged began to make mysterious sounds—always at _____.

5. A Roman _____ had the statue's damaged torso repaired, and, ever since, the statue has been silent.

True or False?

1. Two gigantic statues stand in wetlands east of the Nile River in Egypt. _____

2. The huge statues depict a pharaoh who ruled Egypt long ago. _____

3. One of the colossi lost part of its torso during an earthquake. _____

4. After the earthquake, the statue that had been badly damaged began to make mysterious sounds. _____

5. The Colossus of Memnon continues to make strange sounds at sunrise even today. _____

Unscramble these words from the activity:

1. UETATS _____
2. LUSOSSCO _____
3. THEARAKQUE _____
4. RSOTO _____
5. STERMYSIOU SNDOUS _____

Extension

Why do old houses have lots of odd creaks and make weird noises at night?

Answer Key

1. The Mystery of the Bed of Nails

Solution to the Mystery

Reclining on a bed of nails is an age-old fakir presentation. Spreading out a person's weight over a large surface area provides support without any one point putting too much pressure on the body. Reclining on one nail would cause that nail to sink into the body because all of the person's weight would be concentrated at that one point. Lying down on a bed of many nails spreads the person's weight over a large surface area, so each point is not carrying too much weight. In the related example, the skier does not sink into deep snow, because the skis spread the skier's weight over a large surface area. In the lab, you saw that the book could be supported by tubes of paper because the weight is distributed over six tubes.

Answers to Exercises

Fill in the Blanks

1. Magician
2. Nails
3. Stand
4. Wounds

True or False?

1. False
2. False
3. True
4. True

Unscramble

1. Puncture
2. Wound
3. Nail
4. Fakir
5. Ski

2. The Mystery of the High Wire Walker

Solution to the Mystery

The phenomenon demonstrated in the activity is called center of balance. Center of balance is the point on an object at which it will balance. For a tightrope walker, the center of balance can be improved by using a long pole. This actually places the tightrope walker's center of balance below his body and makes it easier to stay on the rope. As you saw from the lab, as long as the clay is well below the cutout shape, the cardboard figure is very stable on the string and balances well.

Answers to Exercises

Fill in the Blanks
1. Blondin
2. 3 inches
3. Ontario
4. Balance

True or False?
1. True
2. False
3. False
4. False

Unscramble
1. Wire
2. High
3. Balance
4. Walker
5. Fall

3. The Mystery of the Brooklyn Bridge Disease

Solution to the Mystery

This mysterious disease was caused by the extreme depth and pressure under which the sandhogs were working inside the caisson. Working in the caisson for long periods under high pressure and then returning to the surface without decompressing (returning their body gradually to the low pressure at the surface) caused nitrogen bubbles to form in the worker's bloodstream, thus causing immense pain and paralysis. Today we call this "the bends." Though the builders of the bridge never came up with a cure (that came during the twentieth century with the advent of the submarine and decompression chamber), they recognized that it was pressure that was causing the problem. The builders made sure that the workers limited their time inside the caisson, and so they were able to complete the bridge.

In the lab, students learn that gas under pressure (as in a sealed soda bottle) will come out of a liquid when pressure is released.

Answers to Exercises

Fill in the Blanks
1. The Brooklyn Bridge
2. Caisson's disease
3. Great
4. Bubbles

True or False?
1. True
2. True
3. False
4. False

Unscramble
1. Brooklyn
2. Raisin
3. Bridge
4. Pain
5. Gas

4. The Mystery of the Magician's Flame

Solution to the Mystery
The magician is secretly squirting a flammable powder into the air. The igniter and the powder are hidden in his hand. Cornstarch, which comes from corn, is flammable. Dumping the cornstarch on the flame puts out the

flame because it keeps oxygen from reaching the flame. Blowing the cornstarch across the flame, however, spreads out its surface area so there is plenty of oxygen and the cornstarch catches fire. This causes a "blow torch" type of effect, with the particles of cornstarch all lighting at once. There is a chemical that comes from the spore of a fern plant called lycopodium powder. This powder is sometimes called "dragon's breath." It is very flammable and is used on stage and by magicians to create flash effects.

Answers to Exercises

Fill in the Blanks
1. Illusions
2. Fire
3. Goggles
4. Plants

True or False?
1. True
2. True
3. True

Unscramble
1. Plant
2. Straw
3. Flame
4. Cornstarch
5. Illusion

5. The Mystery of the Desert Mirage

Solution to the Mystery

Light travels in a straight line through glass, air, or most transparent materials. When light travels from one medium to another, however, such as from air to water, it gets bent, or refracted. The first activity in this section demonstrated refraction by showing how the light refracted between the air outside the glass and the water in the glass and made the pencil look larger. A desert mirage is an optical illusion that is caused by refraction. In very simple terms, in the desert the light from the sun gets bent when it moves from cooler air in the upper atmosphere into the very warm air near the earth's surface. This bent light causes people to see a portion of the blue sky reflected on the ground. Our brains then take over and imagine that the blue stuff on the ground must be water.

The other activities in the lab demonstrate other kinds of optical illusions. The second activity shows the appearance of a "sausage" between the two index fingers. The third activity shows a "hole" appearing in the hand! All three activities show something that is not—all are optical illusions!

Answers to Exercises

Fill in the Blanks

1. Optical illusion
2. Mirage
3. Sahara
4. Bedoin
5. Refract

True or False?

1. True
2. False
3. True
4. False

Unscramble

1. Mirage
2. Desert
3. Light
4. Sahara
5. Air

6. The Mystery of the Human Cannonball

Solution to the Mystery

The first human cannonball performance in the late 1800s used a spring mechanism to catapult the performer into the air. In our lab we used the elastic as a spring mechanism to simulate this type of cannon. (The longer the elastic loop, the farther the cotton ball would travel.) Later cannons may have used a cylinder inside the cannon powered by compressed air. The performer was loaded into the mouth of the cannon and actually stood on the top of the cylinder. The cannon was primed with compressed air, which when triggered would shoot its occupant into the air. The "boom" sound is for show and has nothing to do with propelling the human cannonball. Gunpowder is not the propellant. Injuries incurred by performers of this stunt are usually caused by missing the target, such as a net or trampoline, not from the cannon itself.

Answers to Exercises

Fill in the Blanks
1. Hugo Zacchini
2. Net
3. Ferris wheels
4. Human cannonballs

True or False?
1. False
2. True
3. False
4. True

Unscramble
1. Catapult
2. Human
3. Elastic
4. Cannon
5. Shoot

7. The Mystery of the Bermuda Triangle

Solution to the Mystery

What you saw from the lab was that ships float because of buoyancy. A ship pushes down on the water with a particular force and the water pushes back with the same force. These forces have to balance for the ship to float. All ships are filled with air. This fact makes them lighter than water (less dense). When you splash water in the boat in the lab, the water fills up the space that should have been filled with air, so the boat sinks. The Bermuda Triangle is an area of intense storms with huge waves that could smash into a ship, thus filling up its air spaces with water and causing it to sink.

Answers to Exercises

Fill in the Blanks

1. Devil's
2. Florida
3. Ships
4. Bermuda Triangle
5. Buoyancy

True or False?

1. False
2. False
3. False
4. True
5. True

Unscramble

1. Bermuda
2. Ships
3. Triangle
4. Cyclops
5. Disappeared

8. The Mystery of the Booming Desert

Solution to the Mystery

Sand is mostly composed of tiny particles of silica, quartz, and other finely ground up rocks and minerals. In between these particles is air. These particles slip and slide when the wind stirs up the sand. Gigantic sand dunes comprise trillions and trillions of sand particles. When the wind causes these dunes to shift or collapse, the colliding sand particles produce a booming sound because a large amount of air is suddenly pushed out from between the sand particles. Sometimes even when there is no wind, a giant dune will collapse under its own weight, thereby producing a boom.

Without the air between the particles of sand, the sand would not slip or slide and there would be no "boom"!

From the lab, you should have discovered that the sand made a noise when it was shaken in the cup. When more sand is added to the cup, the noise is louder. When sand is rubbed between two pieces of paper, it gives a scratchy sound. When water is added to the sand, it fills up the air spaces and the noise is decreased. There is less air space between the sand particles.

Answers to Exercises

Fill in the Blanks

1. Northern Africa
2. Shifting
3. Booms
4. Shakes

True or False?

1. False
2. False
3. True
4. False

Unscramble

1. Sand
2. Boom
3. Sahara
4. Desert
5. Sound

9. The Mystery of the Loch Ness Monster

Solution to the Mystery

The Loch is over 1,000 feet deep and 25 miles long. Visibility in the Loch is only a few feet due to the vegetation suspended in the water. This makes it difficult for investigators to determine whether there is any truth to the stories of a mysterious creature in the Loch. It is also against the law to try to capture or harm Nessie in any fashion. Scientists have tried many different ways of discovering whether there really is a Loch Ness Monster. They have set up twenty-four-hour camera "watches" of the Loch. They have used side-scan sonar devices trailed by small boats navigating the areas where Nessie is most often seen. They have used underwater cameras and underwater listening devices. They have tried scuba divers.

Although sonar and underwater video have produced some unidentified images, there have been no clear pictures taken or other evidence of the so-called monster.

As the students did in the black box activity, scientists have to try to determine the answer by means other than sight alone. So far they haven't found anything in the lake that points to there being a huge creature of some kind living there.

Answers to Exercises

Fill in the Blanks

1. Lake
2. Nessie
3. Fins
4. Dinosaur-like
5. Scientific method

True or False?

1. True
2. True
3. True
4. False

Unscramble

1. Box
2. Nessie
3. Scientific
4. Ness
5. Loch

10. The Mystery of the Flying Rods

Solution to the Mystery

The patterns of iron filings show the invisible lines of magnetic force that are present around all magnets. The earth itself acts as a giant magnet, which is why compasses line up with those invisible lines of force around the earth and point north. The videotape reacted to the small kitchen magnet. Videotape is made of magnetic material. The videos that have been taken of the flying rods have all been filmed with camcorders that use magnetic videotape. It is possible that these effects may be caused by the magnetic tape being exposed to strong lines of force or magnetic materials in the cave. This has yet to be investigated. Exposing a magnetic video- or audiotape to a strong magnetic field will erase whatever is on the tape.

So if it is a magnetic field in the cave that is causing this phenomenon, it can't be very strong.

Answers to Exercises

Fill in the Blanks
1. Midway
2. Parachutes
3. Flying rods
4. North

True or False?
1. True
2. True
3. True
4. True

Unscramble
1. Magnetic
2. Compass
3. Wings
4. Rods
5. Flying

11. The Mystery of the Raining Frogs

Solution to the Mystery

Swirling winds create both tornadoes and waterspouts, similar to the way in which you created the vortex in the bottle by swirling the bottles around. Tornados usually occur during warm weather when the center of a powerful thunderstorm sucks moist air upward. This fast surge of air creates an area of low pressure. The higher-pressure air on the outside of the surge causes the air to revolve faster and faster. If the pressure on the inside of the surge is low enough—and the pressure on the outside is high enough—a tornado will result.

A waterspout begins with a column of rotating air that develops from a cumulus or flat-bottomed cloud over a body of water. Cold air over warm water causes pressure differences that result in a circulating funnel of air that draws water up into it. Waterspouts sometimes pick up frogs and fish from ponds or lakes along with the water. If the waterspout then travels to land, the frogs and fish can fall to the ground. This is how it can sometimes rain frogs!

Answers to Exercises

Fill in the Blanks

1. London, Sineola
2. Tornado
3. 200 mph
4. Vortex

True or False?

1. True
2. False
3. False
4. True

Unscramble

1. Wind
2. Tornado
3. Spout
4. Pressure
5. Vortex

12. The Mystery of the Glowing Ball of Light

Solution to the Mystery

Lightning is a form of static electricity usually caused by a buildup of electrical charges in a storm cloud that discharge into the ground. The ball lightning that appeared to Victoria Mondello was a probably a form of lightning, but scientists are still arguing exactly what ball lightning is made of and why it occurs. The most recent theory is that ball lightning is composed of charged particles suspended in a ball of charged gas. Ball lightning has been known to travel along high-tension wires, telephone lines, fences, and stone walls. Ball lightning is most often seen on farmland and has been reported as appearing out of a cloud, bouncing across a field, and setting haystacks on fire!

The lab demonstrates how static electricity is formed. Rubbing the balloon on your sleeve or on your hair caused it to pick up extra electrons and become negatively charged. When you brought the balloon close to the cup or touched the cup with it, the electrons were transferred to the cup and it became negatively charged. This made the pieces of Styrofoam stick to the plastic cup. Bringing the balloon close to but not touching the cup is called charging by induction. Touching the cup with the balloon is called charging by conduction.

Answers to Exercises

Fill in the Blanks
1. Farm
2. Ball lightning
3. Hole
4. Electrons
5. Static electricity

True or False?
1. True
2. False
3. False
4. False

Unscramble
1. Static
2. Lightning
3. Ball
4. Spark
5. Balloon

13. The Mystery of the Green Flash

Solution to the Mystery

When light passes through a prism or through a film of bubble solution, it separates into the colors of the spectrum—red, orange, yellow, green, blue, and violet (roygbv). Scientists can use spectral analysis to identify unknown substances. Certain substances emit certain colors if light passes through them. It is thought that the Green Flash is caused by sunlight striking the salt water and being refracted into the air as the sun settles below the horizon. The green and blue part of the spectrum is refracted by the water. The blue is absorbed by the air molecules and the green appears as a sudden flash.

Answers to Exercises

Fill in the Blanks

1. Refracted
2. Red, orange, yellow, green, blue, and violet
3. Prism
4. Green

True or False?

1. True
2. False
3. True
4. False
5. True

Unscramble

1. Green
2. Refract
3. Red
4. Reflect
5. Flash

14. The Mystery of Yellow Fever

Solution to the Mystery

From the descriptions of the different cabin conditions you should have figured out the three theories of that time of how yellow fever was transmitted: (1) by something in the air, (2) by contact with people who had the disease (or something they had touched, such as sheets), or (3) by mosquitoes.

Walter Reed's cabin experiment was a controlled experiment. Cabin #1 was the control, which meant that none of the possible contagions could get into this cabin. In cabin #2 there was one variable: the open window. This tested the "bad night air." In cabin #3 the variable was the possibly contagious sheets. In cabin #4 Walter Reed tested his own theory that mosquitoes passed yellow fever from person to person, by putting the mosquitoes inside the net. The fact that the volunteer in cabin #4 was the only one to get yellow fever shows that Reed was correct.

Answers to Exercises

Fill in the Blanks

1. Contagious
2. Liver
3. Walter Reed
4. Controlled experiment

True or False?

1. False
2. True
3. True
4. False
5. True

Unscramble

1. Mosquito
2. Fever
3. Cuba
4. Cabin
5. Reed

15. The Mystery of Greek Fire

Solution to the Mystery

No one knows exactly what Greek Fire was made of but it may have been a chemical reaction that was pressurized. Some historians believe it may have been shot from hollowed out logs that were sealed on one end and open on the opposite end. As you saw in the lab, a chemical reaction can produce great pressure, and the products of the reaction would have nowhere to go but out the open end of the tube. Others say that the chemicals may have been shot by using a siphon device. The chemicals used may have included some type of tar or resin that was quite flammable. It also may have included other chemicals, such as magnesium, that are known to burn under water.

Answers to Exercises

Fill in the Blanks

1. Callinicus
2. Burn
3. Ships
4. Chemical reaction
5. Chemicals

True or False?

1. False
2. False
3. True
4. True

Unscramble

1. Greek
2. Fire
3. Chemical
4. Cannon
5. Ship

16. The Mystery of the Lindow Moss Bog Man

Solution to the Mystery

The apple slice in the lab that was covered in lemon juice did not turn brown. The apple slice that was not covered in lemon juice did turn brown. The acid in the lemon juice prevented oxygen from getting into the apple slices. Oxygen is what makes apples turn brown. The bog is acidic, low in oxygen, and extremely cold. All of these conditions would prevent bacteria from growing and causing the body to decay.

Answers to Exercises

Fill in the Blanks

1. Peat bog
2. 2,000
3. Mummified
4. Acid

True or False?
1. True
2. False
3. True
4. False

Unscramble
1. Bog
2. Mummy
3. Skin
4. Acid
5. England

17. The Mystery of the Vanished Cliff Dwellers

Solution to the Mystery

The Anasazi were an ancient people that took up residence in the four corners (Colorado, Utah, New Mexico, Arizona) about 1200 A.D. and then vanished. Scientists think they may have arrived in this area from farther south on the American continent. The dwellings at Mesa Verde seem to be their only settlement. A combination of drought (lack of water), disease due to overcrowding, and poor sanitation probably brought about the end of this short-lived civilization. The Anasazi were absorbed by the Hopi and other Pueblo cultures of the American Southwest.

The clue you get from the lab results is that the Anasazi's water source may have dried up rather suddenly. In the lab, the chemical, sodium polyacrylate, absorbs the water, forming a slush that remains in the cup when it is turned upside-down. The water disappears!

Answers to Exercises

Fill in the Blanks
1. Colorado
2. Mountains
3. Anasazi Indians
4. Disappeared

True or False?

1. True

2. False

3. False

4. True

Unscramble

1. Anasazi

2. Cliff

3. Dwellers

4. Unsanitary

5. Disappeared

18. The Mystery of Bigfoot

Solution to the Mystery

Unlike pictures or footprints, DNA matching is a definitive method of identifying living things. Though skeptical of Bigfoot, some scientists say they have not been able to identify the DNA from the hair samples supposedly left by the creature. Others have tested mysterious hair samples and found that they were a perfect match for buffalo!

Answers to Exercises

Fill in the Blanks

1. Northwest

2. Hair

3. Sasquatch

4. Bigfoot

5. Picture

True or False?

1. True

2. False

3. False

4. True

Unscramble

1. DNA

2. Sasquatch

3. Forensic

4. Hair

5. Bigfoot

19. The Mystery of Noah's Ark

Solution to the Mystery

If the Ark that has been described in the Bible was really made of wood and in the dimensions estimated, it would break apart in water. Large ships have steel trusses along the keel and steel ribs to support the massive weight of a large vessel. Wood does not have the strength of steel, so it could not be used in this manner. By separating the ship into smaller compartments, however, the support can be maintained for a much larger vessel. In the lab, you demonstrated how individual compartments could be linked together to make for a stronger structure that was able to float and to hold up the paper clips. Noah's Ark could have been as large as described if it was composed of many compartments.

Answers to Exercises

Fill in the Blanks

1. 450, 25, 50

2. Wood

3. Iron and steel

True or False?

1. True

2. False

3. True

Unscramble

1. Noah

2. Ship

3. Ark

4. Steel

5. Compartment

20. The Mystery of Napoleon's Death

Solution to the Mystery

Napoleon became a recluse in the latter months of his life and continually stayed indoors. The green wallpaper in the house where he lived did have small amounts of arsenic in it and could have emitted poisonous vapors in St. Helena's humid climate. Arsenic also could have been in the wine Napoleon drank every day. At least these conditions could have contributed to Napoleon's death. It has also been suggested that Napoleon may have died of stomach cancer. There is no clear evidence that he was intentionally poisoned. Although Napoleon's butler died soon after him, we have no forensic evidence from the butler that would indicate how he died.

Answers to Exercises

Fill in the Blanks
1. St. Helena
2. Arsenic
3. Detect
4. Blood, tissue
5. Butler

True or False?
1. False
2. False
3. True
4. True
5. False

Unscramble
1. Napoleon
2. Arsenic
3. Vapor
4. Helena
5. Humid

21. The Mystery of Lucy's Dinner

Solution to the Mystery

Lucy and others of her kind would have needed protein to survive. Protein can be found not only in meat but also in the bone marrow of animals. Protein is high in iron, which is why the lab results showed that the marrow contained iron. Lucy may have been a scavenger who hunted for the carcasses of freshly killed animals. After the carcasses were left by the large animals, she could have taken the bones, cracked them open, and scraped out and eaten the marrow for a rich protein source.

Answers to Exercises

Fill in the Blanks

1. 3.5 million
2. Upright
3. 65, 3, 4
4. Iron
5. Protein

True or False?

1. False
2. False
3. True
4. True
5. False

Unscramble

1. Lucy
2. Tool
3. Iron
4. Protein
5. Marrow

22. The Mystery of the Burning Oak Tree

Solution to the Mystery

From the lab, you discovered that different kinds of plants produce different types of root systems. Oak trees have extremely deep root systems that connect the trees to the water table. Water is a good conductor of electricity, so the oak tree is hit more often by lightning than other kind of trees.

Answers to Exercises

Fill in the Blanks

1. Oak tree
2. Electricity
3. Deep
4. Shallow
5. Water table

True or False?

1. False
2. False
3. True
4. True
5. False

Unscramble

1. Tree
2. Roots
3. Water
4. Lightning
5. Table

23. The Mystery of the Oak Island Money Pit

Solution to the Mystery

In the first trial of the lab, placing water into the latex tubing slightly pressurizes the latex tube. By placing the free end lower than the container with water, the pressurized tube draws water up and it then runs downhill by gravity into the empty container.

The siphon only works in the first trial. In the second trial, the siphon wouldn't work because the tubing wasn't first pressurized with drops of water. In the third trial, the siphon wouldn't work because the water would have to travel all the way uphill. The Oak Island money pit is set up like a siphon, which continually fills up the pit with water from the ocean.

Answers to Exercises

Fill in the Blanks
1. Nova Scotia
2. Treasure
3. Water
4. Downhill
5. Higher

True or False?
1. True
2. False
3. True
4. False

Unscramble
1. Treasure
2. Pit
3. Oak
4. Siphon
5. Money

24. The Mystery of the Black Death

Solution to the Mystery
The Black Death was caused by a bacteria transmitted by fleas from rats that lived in the cities. In the lab, you studied some predator–prey relationships. When the population of a predator is decreased, then the population of its natural prey increases. When people killed the cats, the rat population increased and even more people got the plague.

Answers to Exercises

Fill in the Blanks
1. One-third
2. Bubonic plague
3. Cats
4. Hunter
5. Hunted

True or False?
1. True
2. True
3. True
4. False
5. True

Unscramble
1. Rats
2. Black Death
3. Prey
4. Predator
5. Plague

25. The Mystery of Galloping Gertie

Solution to the Mystery

The airplane wing demonstrates Bernoulli's Principle. According to this principle, the air rushing over the top and bottom of an airplane wing creates a pressure difference with low pressure on the top and high pressure on the bottom. This gives the wing and the airplane lift. Because the Tacoma Narrows Bridge was built in the shape of an airplane wing, it also experienced lift when the wind rushed over and under it. Eventually, the force of the lift was enough to break the bridge apart.

The lab demonstrates how the pressure differences produce lift. In the first activity, the piece of paper achieves lift when you blow over the top of it because the air moves faster above the piece of paper than below it. In the second activity, the pieces of paper move together because blowing between the two sheets creates an area of low pressure between the pieces of paper. In the third activity, breathing into the funnel causes there to be lower pressure inside the funnel than outside the funnel, so the ping-pong ball is held in the funnel.

Answers to Exercises

Fill in the Blanks
1. Tacoma Narrows Bridge
2. Airplane wing
3. Rocked
4. Collapsed
5. Lower

True or False?
1. False
2. False
3. True
4. True
5. True

Unscramble
1. Gertie
2. High
3. Pressure
4. Wind
5. Tacoma

26. The Mystery of the Oregon Vortex

Solution to the Mystery

Perspective is the key to optical illusions. In Activity 1, your view of the object changes in position because your eyes are a small distance apart. This difference allows your brain to judge depth. In Activity 2, changing the position of the arrow points makes one line appear shorter than the other. When you measured the lines, you saw that they were actually the same size. In Activity 3, when you bring the two fingers close to your eyes, a "sausage" will appear between the fingers. This is caused by your eyes crossing. Again, this is a change in perspective.

The area called the Oregon Vortex is also set up as an optical illusion, playing with perspective to make people "see" things that aren't there.

The vortex is like the slanted room in an old fun house. Everything in a slanted room was built at an angle so that when you walked into the room your perspective would be thrown off, which made it very difficult to keep your balance.

Answers to Exercises

Fill in the Blanks
1. Gold Hill, Oregon
2. The Forbidden Ground
3. Horses (or Ponies)
4. Perspective
5. Optical

True or False?
1. False
2. True
3. True
4. True
5. False

Unscramble
1. Optical
2. Illusion
3. Perspective
4. Vortex
5. Oregon

27. The Mystery of the Taos Hum

Solution to the Mystery
Taos sits on the Rio Grande Fault Line. Many scientists think the hum some people hear is caused by the constant grinding of the fault. The dry conditions of this region may make the hum more audible than in other fault regions. Scientists are still investigating.

The lab shows that dry dirt produces a more audible noise when rubbed between the sheets of paper than does the wet dirt.

Answers to Exercises

Fill in the Blanks

1. Low-pitched
2. Sleeping
3. Dry
4. Crack

True or False?

1. True
2. False
3. False
4. True

Unscramble

1. Noise
2. Taos
3. Continuous
4. Dry
5. Crust

28. The Mystery of Cooking Without Heat

Solution to the Mystery

Making pickles from cucumbers, as you did in the lab, is one form of "heatless cooking." Pickling causes a chemical reaction within the food that is similar to cooking. The reaction causes a molecular change in the cucumber, which affects its taste and texture.

Marinating meat is another form of heatless cooking. The marinade causes chemical changes within the meat. When the meat is actually cooked, it takes less time on a flame because it is partially cooked.

Ceviche is a form of South American cuisine in which fish is marinated in lime or lemon juice, vegetables, and spices. The lemon or lime juice reacts with the raw fish and turns it opaque and firm. Cooking over a flame results in the same reaction but the taste is much different.

Answers to Exercises

Fill in the Blanks

1. Cultures
2. Without heat
3. Energy
4. Acetic acid

True or False?

1. True
2. False
3. False
4. True

Unscramble

1. Heat
2. Salt
3. Cooking
4. Vinegar
5. Cucumber

29. The Mystery of Spontaneous Human Combustion

Solution to the Mystery

There have been hundreds of reported cases of spontaneous human combustion, but no one has proven that it actually occurs. It has been speculated that a person with a high body fat content and alcohol in his or her system could suddenly burst into flames because, like the wax and ethanol in the lab, fat and alcohol are highly flammable. However, although fat may contribute to reducing a body to ashes, it's far more likely that the fire started from something like a lit cigarette than spontaneously.

Answers to Exercises

Fill in the Blanks

1. Ignition
2. Ashes
3. Alcohol

4. Fruits

5. Burns

True or False?

1. False

2. False

3. True

4. True

Unscramble

1. Flammable

2. Alcohol

3. Spontaneous

4. Burn

5. Combustion

30. The Mystery of the Long Island Typhoid Outbreak

Solution to the Mystery

In the typhoid fever outbreak described, Mary Mallon was found to be a "human carrier" of the disease typhoid fever. A "carrier" is someone who is infected without showing any symptoms. Typhoid Mary, as she became known, spread the infection through her handling of food. After it was discovered that Mary caused the outbreak, she was held at a hospital on an island in New York harbor. She was freed on the condition that she would never hire herself out as a cook again. But she returned to being a cook—causing another typhoid outbreak. She was tracked down and sent back to the island where she lived the rest of her life.

In the first lab, a careful examination of the homes shows that Mary M, the cook, was the only person present in all the homes with typhoid. The second lab shows the importance of hand washing in eliminating germs. Mary Mallon, even though a carrier, might have lessened her contagiousness if she had used proper hygiene and washed her hands before handling foods. Today typhoid is treated successfully with antibiotics, but the best prevention is good hygiene.

Answers to Exercises

Fill in the Blanks

1. Long Island
2. Infected
3. Fluorescent
4. Ultraviolet

True or False?

1. False
2. False
3. False
4. True

Unscramble

1. Germ
2. Typhoid
3. Outbreak
4. Washing
5. Disease

31. The Mystery of the Celt

Solution to the Mystery

An ellipsoid is an elliptical or oval shape that is wide at one end and thin at the other end (like a boat). It is the ellipsoidal shape that causes the celt's strange spin. A celt will only spin counterclockwise. The ellipsoidal shape transfers the force you applied in spinning the celt clockwise into a backward spin. The behavior of a celt is complicated and not fully understood. The best guess of scientists is that the forward rotation and the ellipsoid shape sets up a vibration in the celt that causes it to stop but continues to vibrate along its length (it rocks up and down). This vibration and the ellipsoid shape cause the celt to then spin in the opposite direction until gravity and friction cause it to stop.

Answers to Exercises

Fill in the Blanks

1. Tools
2. Gouge wood

3. 1,500

4. Flat

True or False?

1. True

2. False

3. False

4. False

Unscramble

1. Tap

2. Celt

3. Rock

4. Adze

5. Spin

32. The Mystery of the Hot Springs

Solution to the Mystery

In Activity 1, the balloon got smaller in the cold and expanded when it was placed in a warm place. This shows how fluids expand when they are heated. In Activity 2, the water you squeezed out of the sponge simulates how the expanding water gushes quickly to the surface at Hot Springs.

The water from the Hot Springs rises to the surface more quickly than it sinks because the earth gets hotter and hotter the deeper you go. This water becomes hot and expands, which causes it to move back up to the surface. The water that reaches the surface is around 143 degrees F.

Answers to Exercises

Fill in the Blanks

1. Arkansas

2. 143 degrees Fahrenheit

3. 4,000 years

4. Less than a year

True or False?

1. True

2. True

3. True

4. True

Unscramble

1. Hot

2. Cold

3. Arkansas

4. Spring

5. Water

33. The Mystery of Easter Island

Solution to the Mystery

Moving a textbook from one place to another is doing work. Friction makes work harder. Friction is caused when one surface rubs up against another surface. Simple machines make work easier. The lever, pulley, inclined plane, wheel, and axle are all simple machines that are found in early primitive cultures in some form or another. The statues on Easter Island were probably moved by using logs (like the pencils in the lab) or sledges to make work easier. A sledge is a flat platform that is dragged or pushed over the ground (like the newspaper in the lab). Scientists have determined that there were palm trees present on the island at the time the statues were carved. The deforestation of the island and the sudden end to the carving of statues seem to coincide.

Answers to Exercises

Fill in the Blanks

1. Jacob Roggeveen

2. Volcanoes

3. Heads

True or False?

1. False

2. True

3. False

4. True

5. True

Unscramble

1. Volcanic
2. Easter
3. Work
4. Stone
5. Head

34. The Mystery of the Deadly Lake

Solution to the Mystery

When you mix baking soda and vinegar, as you did in the lab, you create carbon dioxide gas. The candle flame needs oxygen to burn. When the carbon dioxide gas fills up the glass, it pushes out all of the oxygen, so the candle flame is extinguished. Carbon dioxide is heavier than air, so it pushes the air up and out of the glass.

Lake Nyos sits on an old volcano. Carbon dioxide from lava beds deep in the earth seeps up into the lake and dissolves in the cold water. Over time the bottom of the lake becomes supersaturated with carbon dioxide. Anything like a small earthquake or a landslide can make the gas suddenly be released from the water and rise to the surface. This is called "outgassing." Animals and humans need oxygen to survive. In 1984, everything around Lake Nyos was asphyxiated (suffocated) when a cloud of carbon dioxide erupted from the lake. Because the gas is heavier than oxygen, it pushed the oxygen away from the area around the lake in the same way the carbon dioxide in the lab pushed the oxygen away from the candle. After the gas erupted, the level of the lake dropped about three feet, showing how much gas was released! Since the accident, scientists have sunk a pipe that stretches from the surface down to a deep section of the lake in hopes to slowly "degas" the lake and prevent buildup of carbon dioxide.

Answers to Exercises

Fill in the Blanks

1. Camaroon
2. Volcano
3. Animal
4. Carbon dioxide

True or False?

1. False

2. True

3. False

4. False

Unscramble

1. Nyos

2. Carbon

3. Deadly

4. Dioxide

5. Vinegar

35. The Mystery of Magnetic Hill

Solution to the Mystery

In the lab, the students experienced some optical illusions. Optical illusions trick the eye into seeing something different from what's really there. The eye is drawn away from the focus point, or something is introduced to change the point of reference.

In Diagram A, the curve of the two arcs and their position make one arc look bigger than the other. When the two arcs are cut out and placed one on top of the other, you realize that they are exactly the same! In Diagram B, the width of the hat brim looks shorter than the height of the hat, but when you measure them you find that they are exactly the same! The eye is tricked by the position and shape of the hat brim.

The secret of Magnetic Hill is that it also is an optical illusion. Because of the hilly landscape around Magnetic Hill, it is hard to tell whether you are going uphill or downhill. The car seems to be moving uphill of its own accord (or because of some mysterious magnetic force) when actually it is just being pulled downhill by gravity.

Answers to Exercises

Fill in the Blanks

1. New Brunswick

2. Magnetic

3. Roll up

True or False?

1. False

2. True

3. False

Unscramble

1. Magnetic

2. Hill

3. Bottom

4. Car

5. Force

36. The Mystery of the C.S.S. *Hunley*

Solution to the Mystery

The crew of the *Hunley* may have run out of air and been unable to surface. They may have used up more oxygen than anticipated because of the excitement and exertion. The candle in your lab used up all the oxygen in the glass and the flame went out when there was none left.

Answers to Exercises

Fill in the Blanks

1. Submarine

2. Eight men

3. Sink

4. Spar torpedo

5. Port

True or False?

1. False

2. False

3. True

4. True

Unscramble

1. *Hunley*

2. Candle

3. Submarine

4. Civil War

5. Confederate

37. The Mystery of the Dancing Stones of Death Valley

Solution to the Mystery

In the winter months the surface of Racetrack Playa can get slick from rain. At night the desert gets very cold and the water freezes into ice. The frozen sand is very slippery. Desert winds would be strong enough to push the boulders around on this very slippery surface. This is where the mysterious tracks come from.

In the lab, the most friction occurs between the clean block and the ramp surface, so this block should travel down the ramp more slowly than the other blocks. The block with motor oil on it should show the fastest time. Motor oil produces the slickest surface. Like the ice in the desert, the oils reduce friction between objects so they can move with less force being applied to them.

Answers to Exercises

Fill in the Blanks
1. 1 mile
2. 125
3. Freezing
4. Move

True or False?
1. True
2. False
3. True
4. False

Unscramble
1. Heat
2. Friction
3. Valley
4. Death
5. Stones

38. The Mystery of Drowning in Quicksand

Solution to the Mystery

It is impossible to sink out of sight in quicksand. You would have to dive head first into the quicksand and really try hard to keep your head down to accomplish this. The human body is less dense than quicksand, so you would float in it. The buoyancy force of the quicksand is more than the weight of the human body pushing on it.

In the lab, the cans of soda float at different levels (or some float and some just sink) because they each have different densities. The sodas with the most sugar in them per volume are more dense because they use more sweetener, and the sweetener makes the soda heavier than water. In diet sodas, the small amount of sweetener is countered by the gas in the can, so the can is lighter than water.

The egg does not float in fresh water because it is more dense than water. However, salt water is more dense than the egg, so when the egg is placed in salt water, it floats.

Answers to Exercises

Fill in the Blanks

1. Drowning
2. Water
3. Buoyancy

True or False?

1. False
2. True
3. True

Unscramble

1. Buoyancy
2. Force
3. Density
4. Float
5. Quicksand

39. The Mystery of the *Hindenburg*

Solution to the Mystery

There have been many theories about what may have caused the *Hindenburg* tragedy, including a bomb, a hydrogen leak, lightning, and common static electricity. The most likely culprit was the extremely flammable fabric cover of the airship. It could have been ignited by static electricity from the storms in the area or any type of stray spark in the interior of the ship, which in turn set off the hydrogen! With the crash of this behemoth, the age of airships ended.

In the lab, you tested the flammability of some of the materials used in the *Hindenburg* and discovered that the aluminum foil did not burn; the wood burned, but took longer to catch fire; and the cotton cloth caught fire very easily.

Answers to Exercises

Fill in the Blanks

1. Airship
2. Zeppelin
3. Hydrogen
4. Helium
5. May 6

True or False?

1. True
2. False
3. True
4. False
5. True

Unscramble

1. Zeppelin
2. Disaster
3. Cotton
4. Explosion
5. Burn

40. The Mystery of the Giant Pictures

Solution to the Mystery
The lab shows how you can use a grid to enlarge a picture quite accurately. Years ago, sign painters used this technique to produce large billboards. People have wondered how the Nazca could have made such large pictures and geometric shapes, and there is some evidence that they might have used a similar grid technique.

Answers to Exercises

Fill in the Blanks
1. Peru
2. Miles
3. Nazca
4. 200, 150

True or False?
1. True
2. False
3. False
4. True

Unscramble
1. Picture
2. Draw
3. Lines
4. Giant
5. Nazca

41. The Mystery of Stonehenge

Solution to the Mystery
Simple machines, such as the lever, the pulley, and the inclined plane, are used to make work easier. As you saw in the lab, it takes less force to pull an object up a ramp (an inclined plane) than to pull the same object straight up. The ancient people who made Stonehenge probably used ropes and ramps made out of dirt to set the huge rocks into place. The dirt ramps were removed after each stone was set into place.

Answers to Exercises

Fill in the Blanks

1. England
2. 28 tons
3. Circle
4. Inclined plane, ramp
5. Spring balance

True or False?

1. True
2. False
3. True
4. True
5. True

Unscramble

1. Ramp
2. Plane
3. Stonehenge
4. England
5. Stones

42. The Mystery of the Dragons of China

Solution to the Mystery

Ancient people who discovered dinosaur and ancient mammal remains in places such as the Gobi Desert believed these fossils were the bones and teeth of dragons. Many of today's most amazing fossil finds come from arid regions of Mongolia in Asia, the American West, and Argentina in South America. These regions were once under, or near, inland seas that lent themselves to the preservation of fossil evidence.

Answers to Exercises

Fill in the Blanks

1. Dragons
2. Stories
3. Fossil

4. Mold

5. Cast

True or False?

1. True

2. True

3. True

4. True

Unscramble

1. Cast

2. Teeth

3. Dragon

4. Bones

5. Fossil

43. The Mystery of the Woman Who Didn't Drown

Solution to the Mystery

Glass #1 remains filled with water. Glass #2 remains filled with trapped air. When glass #2 is placed under and tipped, the air replaces the water in glass #1. Air can be trapped in objects underwater because it does not dissolve in water. The woman survived because she must have been in a pocket of trapped air and was rescued before she used up all the air in the pocket.

Answers to Exercises

Fill in the Blanks

1. *Eastland*

2. Chicago

3. 800

4. Hand

True or False?

1. False

2. True

3. False

4. True

Unscramble

1. Steamship

2. Trapped

3. Eastland

4. Woman

5. Water

44. The Mystery of the Sargasso Sea

Solution to the Mystery

The unique meeting and melding of warm Atlantic currents and winds moving in a circular motion creates a churning action that pushes ocean waters up to form the Sargasso Sea. This is similar to the action you saw in Activity 1 in which the spinning water rose up in the bowl. The waters of this sea are warmer than the waters that surround it because it is fed by the warm Atlantic currents. The warm water moves to the surface inside the moving currents and forms a sort of lens held in place by surface tension, which you demonstrated in Activity 2. Sargassum weed thrives in the warm calm water of the Sargasso Sea. Seasonal weather changes result in this seaweed being especially dense in spring and summer.

Answers to Exercises

Fill in the Blanks

1. Seaweed

2. Summer

3. Currents

4. Warmer

5. Three

True or False?

1. False

2. True

3. True

4. True

5. False

1. Sargasso Sea

2. North Atlantic

3. Seaweed

4. Clockwise

5. Currents

45. The Mystery of the Ice Fences of the Himalayas

Solution to the Mystery

High up in the Himalaya Mountains, the air is cold and has low humidity. Therefore, when it snows high up in the Himalayas, the snow is light and fluffy. It is called dry snow because this snow, when it falls, does not have much moisture in it.

Light, fluffy snow is readily blown by high winds across snowfields and builds snowdrifts in places where physical features of the terrain create turbulence and friction. This is similar to the way you created piles of salt in the activity.

The Himalayan snowdrifts experience some melting in spring and summer, and refreezing in the fall and winter. The freezing-melting-refreezing process creates solid ice. Winds further erode the ice to carve out the pickets, and gravity makes the pickets wider at the base.

Answers to Exercises

Fill in the Blanks

1. Highest

2. 20,000

3. Everest

4. Fields

5. Ten

True or False?

1. False

2. True

3. False

4. True

5. False

Unscramble

1. Mountains

2. Himalayas

3. Ice pickets

4. Mount Everest

5. Fences

46. The Mystery of the Flash Point

Solution to the Mystery

Smoke, which is composed of hot gases and specks of carbon, rises from the candle when the flame is extinguished. Heat from the burning match ignites the column of hot gases and specks of carbon, which are unburned fuel. The smoke acts like a kind of long fuse, and the flame travels down to the wick, which relights the candle.

Fuel, which is anything that can burn, must be heated until enough of it becomes a vapor (a gas or a mixture of gases) before the fuel bursts into flames. When the flash point—the kindling temperature—of the vapor is attained, fire breaks out. When the heat level in a room rises to the kindling temperature of the gases in the air, the gases that fill the room experience flash point, and the room becomes an inferno.

Answers to Exercises

Fill in the Blanks

1. Inside

2. Outside

3. Room

4. Flash point

True or False?

1. True

2. False

3. True

4. True

Unscramble

1. Flash point

2. Fire

3. Water

4. Firefighter

5. Room

47. The Mystery of the Island That Vanished

Solution to the Mystery

Graham Island was unable to support its own weight and fell in on itself. The island collapsed and returned to the sea from which it had risen.

Graham Island was made of very light volcanic rock. Scoria and pumice (volcanic rock) lack strength because they are very light and are filled with holes. These holes are caused by steam and other gases that are trapped when the rock cools and hardens.

In the activities, you can see that bread, which has holes in it like scoria and pumice, can readily be compressed. The pile of brown sugar is also full of air spaces and, like Graham Island, it easily fell apart when you pounded on the tabletop.

Answers to Exercises

Fill in the Blanks

1. 1831

2. Sea level

3. Fire

4. Diameter

5. Disappeared (or Vanished)

True or False?

1. False

2. True

3. True

4. False

5. True

Unscramble

1. Mediterranean Sea

2. Graham Island

3. Disappear

4. Smoke

5. Fire

48. The Mystery of the Circus Queen's Fall

Solution to the Mystery

The metal swivel in the circus queen's loop would have heated up whenever she swung around. This is because friction creates heat, as you saw in Activity 1. When metal is repeatedly heated and then cools, it experiences fatigue. This makes it easy to break. When metal is heated, its molecules separate, and the metal expands. When it is cooled, the molecules move closely together, and the metal contracts. The repeated expansion and contraction of metal causes metallic crystals to form. The crystallized metal is brittle, and continuing stress causes the metal to break like the twist tie in Activity 2.

Answers to Exercises

Fill in the Blanks

1. Aerialist
2. Safety
3. Roman rings
4. Metal swivel
5. Arm

True or False?

1. True
2. False
3. False
4. True
5. True

Unscramble

1. Lillian Leitzel
2. Roman rings
3. Performance
4. Metal swivel
5. Circus queen

49. The Mystery of the Bouncing Cannonballs

Solution to the Mystery

The U.S.S. *Constitution* was built with thick oak timbers and other tough hardwoods. The lower part of her hull was built with a particular kind of live oak that grows only in South Carolina and Georgia.

Balsa wood is soft and extremely light in weight. It is easily compressed, or dented, when struck by a hammer. Pine is sturdy and durable. It will dent when struck, but not as readily as balsa wood. Maple is a tough, close-grained hardwood that resists compression but will dent. Oak, such as red oak, is a hard, tough durable wood that resists compression, but not as well as maple.

Live oak has elasticity and is highly resilient. It has the ability to be stretched or squeezed together—compressed—and return to its original size and shape. Even if it is struck with much impact, as when hit by a cannonball, the live oak will bounce back and regain its shape.

Answers to Exercises

Fill in the Blanks
1. Old Ironsides
2. Commissioned
3. Boston
4. Handling
5. 1812

True or False?
1. False
2. False
3. False
4. True
5. True

Unscramble
1. Old Ironsides
2. Warship
3. Cannonballs
4. Hull
5. Bounced

50. The Mystery of the *Mary Celeste*

Solution to the Mystery

Alcohol is volatile and readily evaporates. Alcohol fumes are combustible (they can burn), and are especially hazardous in a confined space like the cargo hold of a sailing ship. The open barrels on the *Mary Celeste* may have been creating an unsafe situation in which the ship's hold was full of alcohol fumes.

The captain might have panicked, either because of the alcohol fumes or the nonworking pump, or both. He ordered everyone to get into the lifeboat, which then became separated from the ship and probably sank in a storm. There have been many other theories over the years, from mutiny and piracy to alien abduction! But since there was no blood or other sign of a struggle, these other theories seem unlikely.

Answers to Exercises

Fill in the Blanks
1. *Dei Gratia*
2. Alcohol
3. Navigation
4. Hatches
5. Wood

True or False?
1. True
2. True
3. False
4. True
5. False

Unscramble
1. *Mary Celeste*
2. Alcohol
3. Hatch
4. *Dei Gratia*
5. Voyage

51. The Mystery of the Great Molasses Flood

Solution to the Mystery

The unseasonably warm weather for January probably facilitated the fermentation of the molasses in the big tank. Fermentation is a process that produces alcohol and gives off heat. In the heat inside the tank, the 2.3 million gallons of molasses would have expanded and the alcohol vapors given off by the fermentation process would have collected in the tank. Eventually, the pressure of the expanding molasses and gases probably made the tank explode.

The tank may also have been defective. The company that owned the tank had painted the tank brown—probably to conceal leaking molasses.

In Activity 1, you saw how the red substance in the thermometer, which is alcohol, moved up in the tube as the heat increased. This shows how alcohol expands in the heat.

In Activity 2, the cool air in the glass bottle was warmed by heat energy from the hands that gripped the sides of the bottle. The cool air in the bottle expanded but could not escape easily because of the film of water between the rim of the bottle and the coin, which acted like a seal. When the pressure of the expanding air built up sufficiently, the coin was pushed up, and the warm air escaped. The coin then returned to its original position sitting on the rim of the bottle. In similar fashion, the molasses and alcohol vapors in the molasses tank had no way to escape, so the pressure built up until the whole tank exploded.

Answers to Exercises

Fill in the Blanks
1. 1919
2. Warm
3. Molasses
4. Exploded
5. Died

True or False?
1. True
2. False
3. True
4. False
5. False

Unscramble

1. Boston

2. Storage tank

3. Molasses

4. Exploded

5. Flood

52. The Mystery of the Penny That Knows Whether You're a Girl or a Boy

Solution to the Mystery

There is no obvious solution as to why this trick works. It has been theorized that the movements of the suspended penny are the results of the action of muscles in the hand that is holding the string, and that thinking "girl" and "boy" somehow activates these muscles unconsciously.

Answers to Exercises

Fill in the Blanks

1. Circle

2. Line

3. Upturned

4. Know

True or False?

1. False

2. True

3. True

Unscramble

1. String

2. Penny

3. Girl

4. Boy

5. Palm

53. The Mystery of Nauscopie

Solution to the Mystery

M. Bottineau's accomplishments have never been seriously examined by the science community at large, but there is convincing written testimony from the governor of the Isle of France as well as the attorney general, the commissary general of the Navy in the port, and the chief officer of Army engineers that nauscopie is real.

The ships approaching the Isle of France would have created turbulence in the normally clear air. This is similar to the way you created turbulence by blowing at the bottle.

When you blew air at the bottle, the air current split into two streams of air that swept around the curved sides of the bottle and melded into an eddy of churning air, or turbulence. The turbulent air extinguished the flame.

The approaching ships also would have kicked up sea spray into the air, which in the right light could produce colors in the same way that rainbows are made in a sunny sky. M. Bottineau may have been seeing moving colors on the horizon created by the combination of turbulent air and sea spray reflecting the sun's light.

Answers to Exercises

Fill in the Blanks

1. Nauscopie
2. France
3. Ships
4. Time
5. Horizon

True or False?

1. True
2. True
3. False
4. True
5. False

Unscramble

1. Nauscopie
2. Bottineau
3. Ships
4. Horizon
5. Vapors

54. The Mystery of Amelia Earhart's Disappearance

Solution to the Mystery

With cloudy skies and no radio contact, navigation would have been difficult. If an error in navigation occurred during the long flight (2,556 miles from Lae to Howland), even a small deviation would have been magnified greatly as the aircraft flew over the Pacific Ocean. Amelia Earhart's airplane would have missed its mark, used up its fuel, and gone down in the ocean. The diagram from the lab shows how a small error in calculating position could have been magnified over a long distance.

Answers to Exercises

Fill in the Blanks

1. World
2. New Guinea
3. Howland
4. Radio
5. Stars

True or False?

1. True
2. True
3. False
4. True
5. False

Unscramble

1. Amelia Earhart
2. Pilot
3. Airplane
4. Equator
5. Howland

55. The Mystery of the Snake Charmer

Solution to the Mystery

When a cobra fixes its eyes on something that is moving from side to side, the cobra's upper body and head sway from side to side because the cobra has no neck and cannot turn its head. This is similar to the way you had to sway to follow the pencil without moving your neck. The cobra is actually following the movements of the swaying snake charmer, not dancing to the music. The snake can't even hear the music because it has no ears.

Indian snake charmers often remove the fangs of their cobras so that the cobras cannot inject poisonous venom. New fangs, however, can grow to replace the missing fangs. Snake charmers carry an antidote that is used to prevent the poison from taking full effect if the performer is bitten.

Answers to Exercises

Fill in the Blanks

1. Nags
2. Snake charmer
3. Sways
4. Hoods
5. Dance

True or False?

1. True
2. True
3. False
4. False

Unscramble

1. Cobra
2. Snake charmer
3. Flute
4. Dance
5. Poisonous

56. The Mystery of the Abyss

Solution to the Mystery

A hydrothermal vent is a fissure in the ocean floor that seeps water that is at superheated temperatures of up to 400 degrees Centigrade. The tremendous pressure of the water in the Abyss prevents the superheated water from the vents from boiling. The vent forms where the earth's crustal plates are slowly moving apart, and hot magma (liquid rock) is welling up from below. Seawater works its way one or two miles down into the earth, and is enriched with minerals that leach from the hot rock. The seawater then rises, returns to the ocean floor, and forms a vent. Thermal vents range in diameter from one-half inch to more than six feet.

The living things that live in the Abyss are usually found near hydrothermal vents in the ocean floor. In addition to the warm water, chemicals—especially hydrogen sulfide—in the mineral-enriched water from the thermal vents make life possible in the Abyss.

Answers to Exercises

Fill in the Blanks
1. Marianas Trench
2. Ocean
3. 36,198
4. Ocean floor
5. Oxygen

True or False?
1. False
2. True
3. True
4. False
5. False

Unscramble
1. Marianas Trench
2. Abyss
3. Total darkness
4. Water pressure
5. Oxygen

57. The Mystery of the Fejee Mermaid

Solution to the Mystery

The Fejee Mermaid was a hoax. The body and the tail of a large fish; the shoulders, the arms, and the torso of a female orangutan; and the head of a baboon had been sewn together, ingeniously, by a highly skilled taxidermist.

If a hoax like the Fejee Mermaid were attempted today, scientists could use DNA testing to quickly reveal that parts of the "mermaid" come from different animals.

Answers to Exercises

Fill in the Blanks
1. Sailors
2. Dugongs
3. Manatee
4. 1842
5. Sensation

True or False?
1. False
2. True
3. True
4. True
5. False

Unscramble
1. Fejee Mermaid
2. Barnum
3. Sailor
4. Dugong
5. Manatee

58. The Mystery of Vermeer's Camera

Solution to the Mystery

Light travels in straight lines. In a camera obscura, rays of light from the top of the object, or scene, travel through the little round hole and fall on the bottom part of the screen. Light rays from the bottom part of the object, or scene, fall on the top part of the screen. That's why the image of the candle flame appears upside down.

It is believed that in the late 1500s, some artists started using the camera obscura to trace images and make their paintings more realistic. By the 1700s, the camera obscura was made smaller, and was built in a wooden box with a screen of ground glass in it that was semitransparent and displayed clear images.

There are three things in Vermeer's work that suggest that he may have used a camera obscura. His pictures have close-up perspective, which is typical of photography, not painting. Maps that hang on walls in his pictures are actual maps of real places. His painting of soft light, which reflects off metals and ceramics in his pictures, looks like light that has passed through a lens and is not sharply focused. Whether or not he used a camera obscura, Jan Vermeer, the Dutch master, remains one of the greatest artists who ever lived.

Answers to Exercises

Fill in the Blanks
1. Artists
2. Life-like
3. Obscura
4. Camera
5. Images

True or False?
1. True
2. False
3. True
4. True
5. False

Unscramble
1. Camera obscura
2. Light
3. Image
4. Vermeer
5. Artist

59. The Mystery of the Roswell Incident

Solution to the Mystery

The Roswell Incident remains a mystery. The U.S. Air Force reported in 1947 that a weather balloon had crashed in the Roswell area. A crashed weather balloon would have left tin foil on the ground. Tin is not a space age metal. It is a bluish white metal that bends easily and becomes brittle when it is heated. Tin has properties (characteristics) that are different from the properties of the broken pieces of shiny metal that were reportedly found at Roswell. Each metal has its own properties. The lab shows, for example, that different metals behave differently when heated. The aluminum knitting needle expanded twice as much as the steel one.

It was reported that the fragments found at Roswell could not be dented with a 16-lb. sledgehammer. Intensive laboratory testing of the metal debris by the air force supposedly revealed other properties that showed that the broken metal pieces were not like any other known metal or metal alloy (a mixture of metals). But the air force has denied all of these reports, and there is no physical evidence of any space age metal or alien bodies. It is most likely that the people just saw a crashed weather balloon and the later reports became exaggerated.

Answers to Exercises

Fill in the blanks

1. Explosion
2. Rancher
3. Air Force
4. Crash
5. Weather

True or False?

1. True
2. False
3. True
4. True
5. False

Unscramble

1. Roswell
2. New Mexico
3. Crash site
4. UFO
5. Weather balloon

60. The Mystery of the War That Never Happened

Solution to the Mystery

Robert-Houdin's magic chest could not be lifted because of the presence of an electromagnet, like the one you made in the lab, which was hidden under a carpet on the stage.

The iron bolt and the coil of wire make an electromagnet. The electrical current creates an electromagnetic field of force because anything that carries an electric current acts like a magnet. The magnetic field causes the iron molecules in the bolt to line up in an orderly pattern, which creates a magnetic north pole and a magnetic south pole in the iron bolt. When the current was stopped, Robert-Houdin would pick up the chest. But with the current on, the iron plate hidden in the chest stuck to the electromagnet under the carpet and no one could pick up the chest.

Answers to Exercises

Fill in the Blanks

1. Magician
2. Electricity
3. Algeria
4. Stage
5. Chest

True or False?

1. False
2. True
3. True
4. True
5. False

Unscramble

1. Magnet
2. Electricity
3. Electromagnet
4. Iron Bolt
5. Magician

61. The Mystery of the Floating Island

Solution to the Mystery

Marsh gas, which forms in the summer from decomposing plant life, becomes trapped in the peat, which makes up most of the island, and causes the island to float to the surface. When the gas has escaped into the air, the island once again sinks back down into the water. Another name for marsh gas is methane.

In the lab, the baking soda (a base, or an alkali) and the vinegar (an acid) react chemically and generate carbon dioxide gas, which collects on the mothballs. The bubbles of carbon dioxide gas that collect on the mothballs cause the mothballs to rise up to the water's surface. At the surface, the bubbles of gas burst, and the mothballs sink. The sequence of events is repeated until the baking soda and vinegar no longer generate carbon dioxide gas.

Answers to Exercises

Fill in the Blanks

1. England
2. Weeks
3. Same
4. Firm
5. Band

True or False?

1. True
2. False
3. False
4. True
5. True

Unscramble

1. Island
2. Floating
3. Lake
4. Gas
5. Peat

62. The Mystery of the Disappearing Planet

Solution to the Mystery

M. Lescarbault probably saw a big sunspot, a dark, irregularly shaped spot on the surface of the sun, which appeared to move across the face of the sun because of the earth's rotation. A sunspot is a solar magnetic storm.

Answers to Exercises

Fill in the Blanks
1. Black
2. Vulcan
3. Locate
4. 1878
5. Pluto

True or False?
1. True
2. False
3. True
4. False
5. True

Unscramble
1. Lescarbault
2. Planet
3. Astronomer
4. Vulcan
5. Sunspot

63. The Mystery of the *Titanic*

Solution to the Mystery

As you saw in your lab, water expands when it freezes. The volume—the space that the water takes up—increases by slightly more than nine percent when water freezes, but the mass stays the same. Therefore, ice is less dense than water, so it floats. Density is a measure of mass per volume.

As with the ice in your lab, almost 90 percent of an iceberg is underwater. This is because its density is only slightly different from the density of water.

Since almost 90 percent of an iceberg is underwater, it is difficult for a crew to see an iceberg and to appreciate fully the tremendous size of the entire iceberg. The iceberg can extend over a much wider area underwater than is visible above water. The crew of the *Titanic* didn't see the iceberg until it was too late to turn the large ship away.

Answers to Exercises

Fill in the Blanks

1. *Titanic*
2. Unsinkable
3. Glacier
4. Snow
5. Cuts

True or False?

1. False
2. True
3. True
4. False
5. False

Unscramble

1. *Titanic*
2. Iceberg
3. Glacier
4. Ice
5. Floats

64. The Mystery of the Little Georgia Magnet

Solution to the Mystery

Annie Abbott understood how levers work and the concept of center of gravity, the point at which an object's weight balances. To lift a child by the elbows, the child's elbows must be bent and aligned with the center of gravity, with the arms extended straight up. Only a slight adjustment of the elbows—either forward or backwards—makes lifting the child by the elbows impossible.

The act where she asked the men to try to push her backwards depended on the fact that it takes a little time for several men to grip the rod with both hands and begin to push the rod forward—as a team—at the same time. Meanwhile, the performer subtly pushes the rod up and the men respond by pushing the rod down and forward toward the performer. Pushing down and forward reduces the strength of the men's horizontal force toward the performer.

In addition to her understanding of how levers work and the center of gravity, Annie Abbott was strong and well-coordinated, and, no doubt, had an agile mind.

In the lab, you performed some tricks that were similar to Annie Abbott's. When a person is seated, his or her center of gravity is in the seat. The center of gravity must be moved forward in order for the person to stand up. To move the center of gravity forward, the person's head *must* move forward. Light pressure against the seated person's forehead will keep the person from standing up.

A person whose hands are placed against a wall can successfully resist the force of a chain of people who are pushing with all their strength because each person absorbs the force of the person who is immediately behind him or her. There is no cumulative (added together) force of a chain of people. If the person whose hands are placed on the wall can successfully resist the force of the one person who is right in back of him or her, then that person can resist the efforts of the entire chain of people.

Answers to Exercises

Fill in the Blanks
1. Georgia
2. Eyes
3. Elbows
4. Backwards
5. Unable

True or False?
1. True
2. False
3. True
4. True
5. False

Unscramble

1. Annie Abbott

2. Transfer

3. Magnetic power

4. Lift

5. Little Georgia Magnet

65. The Mystery of the Firewalkers

Solution to the Mystery

It has been suggested that firewalkers experience a mental, perhaps semi-hypnotic, state that makes them insensitive to pain. It has also been suggested that a firewalker's feet are heavily callused so that they resist injury and pain.

It is also possible that the heated stones are, in fact, slaggy cinders that do not heat sufficiently to burn the feet. Firewalkers may pour methylated spirits, ethyl alcohol denatured with methanol, in the shallow pits, which are lined with beds of sticks and twigs and covered with the cinders. The burning bundles of wood and the alcohol would give off light and make the stones seem to glow, but they wouldn't make them very hot.

In the lab, the glow stick, necklace, or bracelet and the fluorescent lamp simulate the stones that glow without heat. In a glow stick, the chemicals are mixed when the glow stick is shaken. A chemical reaction occurs and the glow stick gives off light. In a fluorescent lamp, ultraviolet light rays strike a mineral powder called a phosphor that coats the inside walls of the fluorescent tube, and the phosphor fluoresces, or glows. Neither of these reactions gives off much heat.

Answers to Exercises

Fill in the Blanks

1. Barefoot

2. Pain

3. Burning

4. Tahiti

5. India

True or False?

1. True
2. True
3. False
4. True
5. False

Unscramble

1. Firewalkers
2. Heated stones
3. Shallow pit
4. Fire
5. Barefoot

66. The Mystery of the Human Fly

Solution to the Mystery

Harry H. Gardiner was strong and athletic. He used his fingers to find crevices and holds between the bricks and the big stone blocks. He wore tennis shoes so that his feet would be less likely to slip as he climbed the face of the tall building.

Daniel Goodwin used suction cups and metal clips for support when he climbed the face of the 110-story Sears Tower, which is covered in smooth glass.

Answers to Exercises

Fill in the Blanks

1. Fly
2. Detroit
3. Majestic
4. 211
5. Sears

True or False?

1. True
2. False
3. True
4. False

Unscramble

1. Human Fly
2. Majestic Building
3. Skyscraper
4. Climb
5. Crowd

67. The Mystery of the Mummy's Curse

Solution to the Mystery

In 1986, Dr. Caroline Stenger-Phillip, a French physician, stated that it is very likely that colonies of mold had grown on the fruits that were stored in Tutankhamen's burial site. Mold spores in the air would have been inhaled by people who entered the burial site. The spores could have caused allergenic reactions in some people, which resulted in their deaths. Others feel that the deaths were purely coincidental.

Answers to Exercises

Fill in the Blanks

1. Egypt
2. Died
3. Burial
4. Evil
5. 1922

True or False?

1. False
2. True
3. True
4. True
5. False

Unscramble

1. Archaeologist
2. Tomb
3. Mummy
4. Curse
5. Cairo

68. The Mystery of the Floating Lights

Solution to the Mystery

When air cools, rock that was warmed by the sun's rays is chilled and contracts. It is possible that the cooling forms a crack, or a fissure in the rock, and that as the rock cracks, it creates a series of tiny bursts of intense light that can be seen at night.

As you can see from the lab, while a crystal sugar tablet is being broken it emits a little burst of light that can be seen in the dark. This is similar to what might be causing the dancing lights.

The unusual levels of electromagnetic energy, coupled with seismic activity and the movement of fault lines, might also create bursts of intense, white light. Bursts of light that follow a fault line, one flash after another, in the dark could look like a single light gliding in the air above the ground.

It is possible that ancient peoples observed the strange lights. They might have believed that the ground where the lights had been seen was holy and special, and that is why they built monuments on these sites.

Answers to Exercises

Fill in the Blanks
1. Lights
2. Monuments
3. Carnac
4. Energy

True or False?
1. True
2. False
3. False

Unscramble
1. Floating lights
2. Stonehenge
3. Stone monuments
4. Carnac
5. Electromagnetic energy

69. The Mystery of the Giant Squid

Solution to the Mystery

The deeper you go in the ocean, the higher the water pressure. Giant squids, which have long gills, are able to take in oxygen from air dissolved in water more efficiently in very deep water where water pressure is high. In warmer, shallower water, where the pressure is low, giant squids seem to have circulation and breathing problems.

In Activity 1, you observed that water pressure is different at various depths. The longest stream of water coming from the bottom hole in the milk carton showed that the deeper the water, the stronger the water pressure.

In Activity 2, you saw that pressure can keep a gas dissolved in water. When you took the cap off the bottle, the pressure was released and bubbles of gas rose out of the water. Squids may experience something like "the bends" (which we read about in Activity 3) when they are in shallow water. Gases that are normally dissolved in their bloodstream because of the great pressure in deep water may start to be released, causing the animal pain and distress.

Answers to Exercises

Fill in the Blanks
1. Squid
2. 75
3. Catch
4. 18
5. Shallower

True or False?
1. True
2. True
3. True
4. False
5. False

Unscramble
1. Giant squid
2. Tentacles
3. Shallow water
4. Ocean
5. Beak

70. The Mystery of the Singing Statue

Solution to the Mystery

When the colossus to the north lost its upper torso, a significant fissure, or crack, was created in the stone statue. It is likely that heat exchanges were responsible for the sounds that came from the singing statue. The cold night air of the desert probably made the stone in the fissure contract. At sunrise, rays of sunlight would have quickly heated the stone and the stone expanded. The movement of the stone sides in the fissure would have caused vibrations in the air inside the fissure, which could be heard as strange sounds. The fissure's stone surfaces rubbing against each other would also have produced sounds.

In Activity 1, you saw how a rock can be affected by heat exchanges. When the teacher poured boiling water on the frozen flint, it broke into pieces. The sounds of cracking stone and the noisy bangs of breaking rock could be heard. The outer layers of the flint were heated and expanded more quickly than the inside of the rock, and the resulting stress caused the flint to burst.

In Activity 2, you observed how friction, created by the sliding movement of your fingertip over the moist rim of the glass, caused vibrations to occur in the glass. The vibrations were transmitted to the air, and a bell tone was heard.

Answers to Exercises

Fill in the Blanks
1. Statues
2. Weighs
3. Earthquake
4. Sunrise
5. Emperor

True or False?
1. False
2. True
3. True
4. True
5. False

Unscramble

1. Statue
2. Colossus
3. Earthquake
4. Torso
5. Mysterious sounds

References

Booth, J. *The Big Beast Book.* Boston: Little, Brown, 1988.

Brooks, P. *Invaders From Outer Space: Real-Life Stories of UFOs.* New York: DK, 1999.

Bull, A. *Flying Ace: The Story of Amelia Earhart.* New York: DK, 2000.

Cobb, V., and Darling, K. *Bet You Can! Science Possibilities to Fool You.* New York: Avon, 1983.

Concise Columbia Encyclopedia, J. S. Levey and A. Greenhall (eds.). New York: Columbia University Press, 1983.

Delmar Press. *The Best of Wonder Science.* Albany: Delmar, 1997.

Donkin, A. *Zeppelin: The Age of the Airship.* New York: DK, 2000.

Dubowski, M. *Titanic: The Disaster That Shocked the World!* New York: DK, 1998.

Fisher, J. *Paul Daniels and the Story of Magic.* London: Jonathan Cape, 1987.

Gardner, M. *Science Puzzlers,* 2nd ed. New York: Scholastic, 1964.

Glubok, S. *Discovering Tut-ankh-Amen's Tomb.* Abridged and adapted from Carter, H., and Mace, A. C., *The Tomb of Tut-Ankh-Amen.* New York: Macmillan, 1968.

Harrington, S. J., and Harrington, H. T. "How the Annie Abbott Act Was Performed." *The Linking Ring—Official Publication of the International Brotherhood of Magicians,* June 2003, *83*(6), 50–53.

Kunhardt, P. B., Jr., Kunhardt, P., III, and Kunhardt, P. W. *P. T. Barnum: America's Greatest Showman.* New York: Knopf, 1995.

Lauber, P. *Famous Mysteries of the Sea.* New York: Thomas Nelson, 1963.

Lord, W. *The Night Lives On,* 2nd ed., rev. New York: Jove Books (Berkley Publishing Group), 1987.

Ontario Science Centre, *Scienceworks: 65 Experiments That Introduce the Fun and Wonder of Science.* Toronto: Ontario Science Centre, 1990.

Owen, D. *Police Lab: How Forensic Science Tracks Down and Convicts Criminals.* Buffalo: Firefly Books, 2002.

Popelka, S. *Super Science with Simple Stuff!* Palo Alto: Dale Seymour, 1997.

Puleo, S. *The Dark Tide: The Great Molasses Flood of 1919.* Boston: Beacon Press, 2003.

Reader's Digest. Edited and designed by Dorling Kindersley Ltd. *Facts & Fallacies.* New York: Reader's Digest Association, 1988.

Reader's Digest. *Family Encyclopedia of American History.* New York: Reader's Digest Association, 1975.

Spangler, S. *Taming the Tornado Tube.* Englewood, CO: Wren, 1995.

Taylor, R. L. *Center Ring: The People of the Circus.* New York: Doubleday, 1956. ("Lillian Leitzel" first appeared in *The New Yorker* magazine, April 21 and 28, 1956.)

Van Cleave, J. *201 Awsome, Magical, Bizarre, & Incredible Experiments.* Hoboken, NJ: Wiley, 1994.

UNESCO. *UNESCO Source Book for Science Teaching.* Paris: United Nations Educational, Scientific and Cultural Organization, 1960.

Wallace, J. *Turning Point Inventions: The Camera.* New York: Atheneum, 2000.

Wiese, J. *Detective Science: 40 Crime-Solving, Case-Breaking, Crook-Catching Activities for Kids.* Hoboken, NJ: Wiley, 1996.

Wiese, J. *Ancient Science: 40 Time-Traveling, World-Exploring, History-Making Activities for Kids.* Hoboken, NJ: Wiley, 2003.

Williams, A. R. "Modern Technology Reopens the Ancient Case of King Tut." *National Geographic,* June 2005, *207*(6), 2–21.

Index

Mauritius, 203
Mediterranean Sea, 148
Mesa Verde, Colorado, 52, 236
Metal, tired, 152
Methane gas, 190–192, 278
Methanol, 282
Michigan City, Indiana, 135
Midway, New Mexico, 30
Mold, 210, 284
Molecular change, 246
Mondello, Victoria Mignotte, 36, 231
Mount Everest, 142
Mummy's curse, 209–211; solution, 284

N
Napoleon's death, 62–64; solution, 239
Native Americans, 84
Nauscopie, 166–168; solution, 270
Navigation error, 271
Nazca valley, Peru, 126–128
Neanderthal man, 67
Nepal, 142
"Nessie." *See* Loch Ness Monster
Neutrons, 36
New Brunswick, Canada, 111
New Mexico, 30, 32
Newfoundland, 197
Niagara Falls, New York, 4
Niagara Falls, Ontario, Canada, 4
Nile River, 218
Nitrogen bubbles, 223
Noah's Ark, 58–61; solution, 238
Noonan, Fred, 169–172
North Atlantic Ocean, 138
North magnetic pole, 31

Northern Africa, 24
Nova Scotia, Canada, 72

O
Oak Island money pit, 72–75; solutions, 241–242
Observatory of Paris, 193
Old Ironsides, 154–156
Optical illusion, 14, 86, 225, 244–245, 253
Oregon Vortex, 84–86; solution, 244–245
Outgassing, 252
Oxygen, 91, 114, 223, 224, 235, 252, 286

P
Panama Canal, 45
Parachute jumpers, 30
Peat bog, 235
Penicillin, 211
Peru, 126–128
pH scale, 51
Philippines, 175
Pickling, 246
Pilings, 8
Plesiosaur, 27, 29
Population balance, 76
Predator-prey relationship, 76, 77, 242–243
Prism, 39, 40
Protein, 65–67, 240
Protons, 36
Pueblo cultures, 236
Puget Sound, Washington, 80
Pulley, 251
Pumice, 148, 264

Taos, New Mexico, 87, 88
Tibet, 142
Titanic, 197–199; solution, 279–280
Tornado, 35, 230
Tornado Tube, 33
Trinidad, 203
Turbulence, 270
Tutankhamen, King, 209–211, 284
Typhoid fever, 248–249
Typhoid Mary, 248–249

U

UFO (unidentified flying object), 184
United States Air Force base (Roswell, New Mexico), 184–186, 276
U.S.S. *Constitution,* 154–156; solution, 266
U.S.S. *Cyclops,* 21, 23

V

Vanished cliff dwellers, 52–54; solution, 236
Vanishing island, 148–150
Vermeer, Jan, 181–183; solution, 274–275
Videotapes, 31

Vinegar, 46, 91, 109, 252, 278
Volcanic rock, 264
Vortex, 35, 230, 245
Vulcan, 193

W

War of 1812, 154
War that never happened, 184–189; solution, 277
Water pressure, 214, 286
Water table, 241
Waterspouts, 33, 35, 230, 231
Waterloo, battle of, 62
Western Electric Company, 135
Wheel, 251
Wobblestones. *See* Celts
Woman who didn't drown, 135–137; solution, 260

Y

Yellow fever, 42–45; solution, 233–234
Yellow Fever Commission, 42

Z

Zacchini, Hugo ("Human Cannonball"), 18, 20
Zacchini, Mario, 18, 20
Zeppelin, 123